CW00751715

SEX&DRUGS &SAUSAGE ROLLS

GRAHAM GARRETT
AND CAT BLACK

CONTENTS

First published in 2015 in Great Britain by Face Publications.

www.facepublications.com

A catalogue record of this book is available from the British Library.

ISBN 9780955893049

Written by Graham Garrett & Cat Black
Photography by Adrian Franklin
Designed by Anthony Hodgson
Edited by Jeannie Swales

Printed and bound in China by 1010 Printing International Ltd.

Graham is one of those people who grab life
with the gusto and enthusiasm of a master
has a unique ability to make music with
chef who first worked for me on the English

write his own story with food. He quickly
order reserved for the detail-obsessed and
temple of their passion. He started his life
is now, once again, a god in his second
skilful and simple, cooking from the heart
morsel; I can see much of myself in his work
the candle at both ends as I worked hard and
my passion and sense of duty never waned
and accolade, the highest in our industry
In the day of the pot noodle celebrity chef
the dinner 'quickie' over the bucolic methods
all about. Adhering to invisible and sometime
exciting and seeing others rise to meet them
man. Some people work hard at being rock

by the 'proverbials' and attack any project
Whether it be a drum kit or drumstick he
whatever he tries his hand at. He's a great
Garden restaurant and eventually left to

CHARD-CORRIGAN

joined the ranks of Michelin chefs, a culinary
maniacal individuals that sacrifice all at the
as a successful drummer in the eighties and
incarnation. Eating at his hands is honest,
He is clever and you can taste it in every
Many who know me will tell you that I burnt
partied even harder; however, like Graham,
Achieving Michelin stars is a great honour
however, it doesn't make a successful chef.
who looks more than he cooks, favouring
of the past, keeping your nerve is what it's
unreachable standards is what makes it
is what I live for. This book is about such a
stars: Graham Garrett was born one.

THERE ARE THINGS I'VE DONE
THAT I'M PROUD OF. IT'S ALL GOOD
AND IT'S ALL RELATIVE

INTRODUCTION

By CAT BLACK

In August 2012 I left London, the city of my birth, to move to Kent, to the bottom of a lane, with sheep my new neighbours. As a food writer, and a mixed race woman, London suited me down to the ground. Its melting pot culture and thriving food scene was a joy. So it was with some trepidation that I swapped that 24/7 multi-racial hub for 9-5, closed-on-Sundays, English living. It would be all right if I found good food. Boy, did I find good food! In the quality and abundance of Kentish produce, and in the dining room of a chef who could cut it anywhere on the world stage, but happened to be down the road.

That September I had a booking at The West House in Biddenden. I had seen Graham on Great British Menu earlier that year, and been inevitably struck by his humour, his humility, and just how damn delicious his food looked!

Unlike the pilgrimage that many make to this beautiful little corner of the Weald, I was in a rental ten minutes away. I had driven past the dark-beamed 16th century weaver's cottage a few times. Like many of Biddenden's stunning early buildings it is on the high street, the route through to Ashford. Inside I was charmed. This is somewhere instantly comfortable, full of character but informal, much like the fantasy pub that Graham wanted but never quite got his hands on.

The whole meal exceeded expectations, and my relief at finding such food so near my new home was palpable. This was not just a great local restaurant, it was a great restaurant full stop. I particularly remember a chowder, deep, creamy and fishily full-flavoured, with a perfect muffin alongside. I am a bread obsessive, and an ability to bake is something I value highly.

A tall, handsome young man greeted us on arrival and served us with quiet charm throughout. As a finishing note he brought out two superb chocolates on a little slate.

I recognised them at once as the work of Damian Allsop, one of the world's great chocolatiers, a friend, and whose work had just been awarded multiple gold medals in the International Chocolate Awards, of whose Grand Jury I am a member. My pleasure on seeing the chocolates burst out, and my professional interest in it all was then revealed to the young man, who turned out to be Jake Garrett. A couple of moments later Jake reappeared with an invitation to come and meet Dad.

I found Graham in his modest kitchen, already hard at work on prep for that evening. The West House kitchen was then, and remains to me, a miraculous place. I do not understand how so few, in so small a room, can produce such wonder. It is talent, instinct, palate and focus, I guess. The real brilliance is in the man, not the kit or the gloss of his acres of stainless steel, but the heart and soul, the simplicity and the detail. Graham knows what he is doing, and therein lies deep joy.

That afternoon, while he effortlessly eased and tweaked tortellini into elegant rows full of promise, I perched on a prep bench opposite and we began to talk. We started with Damian, who, it turned out, is a mutual friend, then chocolate and on. Food bonds, and it is a great leveler: age, gender, background and experience fall away. The afternoon became evening, at which point more pressing tasks demanded we part company.

We are a few years on now, and we have shared, obsessed and chuckled over life, the universe and food. I have cooked for Graham at my house; cooking for a Michelin-starred chef is scary, then quite normal, when you realise they just need to eat like anyone else, and are quite grateful to have someone else do it for once.

I have eaten with Graham in various London haunts; which has been hilarious, and hugely informative, as he is straight as a die about where to go, what to order and not too shy to tell it like it is. And of course I have been allowed into the inner sanctum of his magical kitchen.

In early 2014 Adrian, our photographer, suggested to Graham that he do a book. It wasn't the first time, and Graham had always shied away from such a gesture of prominence. He thought the whole proposition rife with risks of arrogance and self-indulgence. But Graham loves books, and his library of food and recipe books is a treasure trove. How could he not want to add his own volume to this? So many of his contemporaries were doing books, and in seeing what they'd done, what was possible, what he might want to do, it all started to seem a better idea. He had also made his peace with his past life behind a drum kit, and didn't mind telling that story, provided he could say it his way.

But how would he manage to write it? He'd need a writer. Which is where I came in, and our friendship took a more professionally productive turn for a while. This book is the result, the insight into a life most extraordinary, the distillation of many hours spent at my kitchen table, perched on that prep bench, listening with dropped jaw to the young man's scrapes and near misses, to the how and why a marriage of ingredients results in bliss.

Always one to mock any tendency to get too pretentious about food, Graham cannot hide his passion for it. The arrival of the new season's strawberries, or a bucket of the pig's blood with which he makes his own black pudding, elicit an outpouring of ideas and renewed excitement. Descriptions of dishes are simple on the menu, precise and eloquent from the man himself.

More often than not when I visit I am asked to taste the latest chocolate he is working on. Making his own chocolates, since Damian relocated to his wife's native Catalonia, is another example of the rigour Graham brings to his menu. There is nothing on it, from the bread, to the charcuterie, to the pickles and Eccles cakes served with the cheese, that is not made in-house. I eat at The West House as often as budget and waistline will allow; I have been known to be there three weeks in a row. I have never seen the same menu twice. I have never, give or take one or two signature dishes the removal of which would get him lynched, seen the same dish twice. I simply do not know how he does it.

That is the mark of a great artist to me. That when you look at their work, whether it is a poem, a drawing, a song or a plate or food, whether it is complex, or startlingly simple, it retains some mystery as to its creation. The method isn't in evidence, it doesn't dominate the experience, in fact it melts away to allow for a pure and happy experience of the thing itself.

As a writer, and an artist, I understand the act of creation. I live and breathe it. But to be a chef is a particularly dedicated form of creativity. You have to create anew daily, multiple times a day, and watch your creations disappear. Quite some labour of love.

Graham loves food. He has been a star, won a star, and yet is utterly down to earth. I am lucky to count him as a friend. It has been a laugh-out-loud privilege and an honour to record his story and his food and help him bring it to these pages.

BABYHOOD

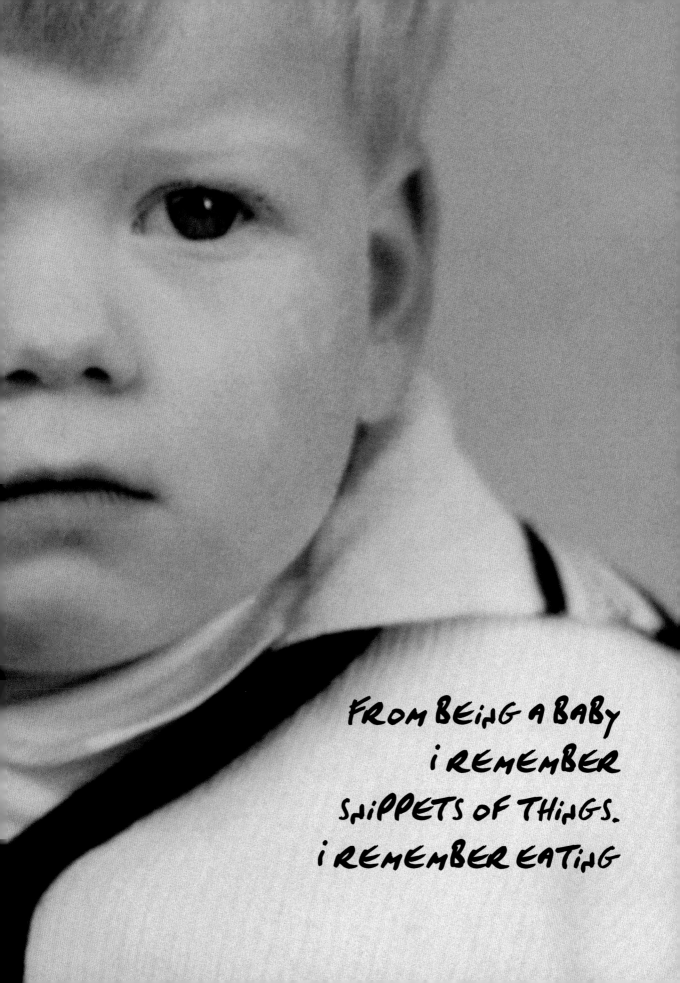

FROM BEING A BABY
i REMEMBER
SNIPPETS OF THINGS.
i REMEMBER EATING

"We were living in Kenton Road, Victoria Park, Hackney. We lived upstairs, and the man I thought was my granddad lived downstairs."

I was born in Hackney Hospital, so I was probably brought from the hospital round the corner to that flat. I don't remember our flat, I don't remember the upstairs. But I remember his kitchen, going into his lounge, I remember his chair, the decor, and I can smell it.

My Dad's dad had died when he was a baby, when he was really young. This guy's name was Jeff, and he was my Nan's ex-husband, from after my Dad's father died, and before she married my Uncle Alf. He was a lovely old boy. Although one day his wife had turned up. Turns out he was a bigamist as well. He had a wife in Holland.

His full name was Robert William Jefferson, he'd been a great football player in England, and then went on to manage teams in Holland when he stopped playing.

But when I was little, he was masquerading as my granddad. I was literally a baby, he was granddad to me.

Jeff used to look after me, during his lunch break, while my Mum was at work, round the corner. He'd always have a frying pan on his stove that was about an inch thick with set lard. He used to cook with that. He used to make big doorsteps of fried bread in his pan of fat. Real heart-clogging stuff. I remember the taste, that thick slice of fried bread. And because of his Dutch connections he always had Dutch butter. It was in a silver wrapper, and everyone else had margarine. This was the early sixties, so that was quite a thing. I'd never heard of Lurpak, that's probably what it was. That taste, that very white, unsalted butter. And the other thing he used to do is poach smoked haddock in milk, which to this day is a favourite dish of mine, with poached eggs.

Jeff used to make lunch for himself, then he'd sit down. He had one of those chain watches in his waistcoat. He used to sit in his chair, then set his watch for half an hour, an hour or whatever. I'd sit on his lap and go to sleep. I always remember those lunch-breaks. It was the food, it was the smells.

Dripping is what you had, bread and dripping for tea. At Christmas time, there was turkey dripping. My Mum used to cook the turkey the night before. When I say the night before I mean she used to cook it for the whole night! She used to set her alarm hourly to get up and baste it. That's how people of my Mum's generation did it. It was that whole fear about it not being cooked. It was ridiculous. You got this dried-out bird the next day. They would render so much fat and juices out of it, there'd be no meat juices left in the bird, they'd all be in the roasting tray. The same was done at Sunday lunch, the beef was dry as anything, but you would have loads of dripping. You'd put that in the fridge to set, so you would have the jelly underneath and the fat on top. You could have that on bread. It was better than the turkey or the beef. Bread and dripping was quite a big deal. That's what you lived on through the week.

THOSE ARE THE VERY
EARLiEST memories

"Flavours like that stick with you. That butter, the haddock, the fried bread. And in those days a pan like that didn't get washed up, it was just put to the side, and it would set. The eggs and bacon would go in the next day, and regenerate it. Same as if you made a stew, you didn't make a stew for a day, you made it for a week."

DRIPPING

Ingredients: makes roughly 1 kilo

1 kilo pork back fat
20g of fresh thyme
butter
fine sea salt
Espelette or Aleppo pepper

To make the dripping, cut the pork fat into smallish pieces and put in a small roasting tin or casserole pot along with the thyme, stalks and all. Roast at around 180°C until the fat has completely rendered. This will take between 45 minutes and an hour, but be careful not to burn it. You'll be left with a lot of oil and some very small shrivelled bits of brown stuff resembling crackling.

Pass the rendered fat through a fine sieve and leave to cool until it starts to solidify but is still soft. If it sets too hard, re-warm it slightly and let it cool again. It needs to be soft white lard.

Weigh your fat and put it in the bowl of your mixer with an equal quantity of soft butter. For every 100g of combined butter and lard add 2.5g of salt. Whisk the mix until it turns completely white and fluffy.

To serve, spread on bread or toast. Sprinkle with a little extra sea salt and pepper flakes.

WHEN I WAS WORKING OUT A METHOD FOR THE DRIPPING TO SERVE IN THE RESTAURANT I FOUND THAT ADDING BUTTER REALLY HELPS TO KEEP IT SMOOTH

BUTTER

IT SUDDENLY OCCURRED TO ME THAT WE USE AN AMAZING DAIRY AND WE MAKE EVERYTHING ELSE OURSELVES, MAKING BUTTER IS A SIMPLE PROCESS, WHY WEREN'T WE MAKING THE BUTTER TOO?

Ingredients: makes roughly 500g

1 litre crème fraîche
10g flaked sea salt

To make the butter, using a food mixer, whisk the crème fraîche until stiff. Reduce the speed and continue to whisk until it separates into solids and liquid. Strain off the liquid through a fine sieve, and store in the fridge for later use as buttermilk, see page 26.

Rinse the butter in a bowl of cold water, then squeeze as much moisture out as possible with your hands before returning to the mixer. Using the beater attachment on a slow speed, add the salt then carry on working the butter until the salt is evenly distributed.

You can now form the butter into blocks, wrap in cling film or greaseproof paper and chill it in the fridge until needed.

BUTTERMILK

Ingredients: makes roughly 1/2 litre

leftover liquid whey from the butter recipe, on page 24
100g live yoghurt
50g whipping cream

To make the buttermilk, whisk everything together. Job done.

Chill it in the fridge until needed.

You can use the buttermilk for the treacle soda bread recipe on page 218 and the milk and honey recipe on page 270.

WE WERE BUYING BUTTERMILK FOR SODA BREAD AND VARIOUS OTHER RECIPES. IF YOU MAKE YOUR OWN BUTTER YOU'RE LEFT WITH TONS OF WHEY, AND IT'S EASY TO TURN IT INTO BUTTERMILK

WARM-SMOKED-HADDOCK, BACON-DRESSING, PEA-SHOOTS

THiS DiSH HAS BEEN WiTH US FOR THE DURATiON OF THE RESTAURANT iN ONE GUiSE OR ANOTHER. i HAVE DONE iT WiTH ROCK SAMPHiRE, BUT CURRENTLY DO iT WiTH PiCKLED SEA PURSLANE

Ingredients: serves 6

6 quail eggs
1 large smoked haddock fillet,
   undyed
a small handful of pea shoots

Pickled sea purslane, or rock samphire

as much purslane or rock
   samphire as you can gather
200ml white wine vinegar
100ml water
10g fine sea salt
15g yellow mustard seeds
50g golden caster sugar

Bacon dressing

25g golden caster sugar
10g light brown sugar
75g water
50g white wine vinegar
1 large free range egg and 1 yolk
30g Dijon mustard
5g salt
250g rapeseed oil
juice of 1/2 lemon
3 rashers of dry cured streaky
   bacon, roughly 5mm thick

To make the pickled sea vegetables, pick through the purslane or samphire discarding any stalks and woody bits, then rinse in cold water. Bring everything else to the boil in a pan, and then pour over the sea vegetables. This can be stored in jars and chilled in the fridge.

To make the bacon dressing, heat the sugars, water and vinegar in a pan until all the sugar has dissolved.

Put the egg, yolk, mustard and salt into a food processor or blender. With the motor running, start to pour in the rapeseed oil very, very slowly. You can go a little quicker once it starts to thicken. When all the oil is in, add the lemon juice. You should now have a thick and luscious mayonnaise. Transfer to a mixing bowl then whisk in enough of your vinegar, a little at a time, to give you a thin salad cream consistency.

Cut the bacon into small lardons and fry until crisp. Reserve the crispy bacon, and whisk the resulting bacon fat into your dressing.

Bring a small pan of water to the boil then boil the quail eggs for exactly 2 minutes and 20 seconds before removing to iced water. Very carefully peel the soft boiled eggs and keep to one side.

To serve, slice the haddock into the thinnest, longest slices you can manage, and lay them, without overlapping, onto a baking tray. Place the tray under a hot grill or in a hot oven for no more than 20 seconds, until the fish is warm and just about to turn opaque. Divide the fish between 6 warmed plates, drizzle with a little of the dressing and scatter pickled sea vegetables and pea shoots over the fish followed by the crispy bacon. Cut each egg in half lengthways and place on top before drizzling more dressing over.

BOYHOOD

AS A KID I WOULDN'T EAT ANYTHING

"I was one of those really fussy kids. I maintain that my Mum is to blame for a lot of that."

If you asked what's for dinner, she'd answer sausages or whatever. But when she used to say wait and see, she might as well just have said liver! Wait and see means liver, because she knew that I hated it. One of the reasons I think I hated liver is that she would do all kinds of things to get me to eat it. She'd fry it, she'd casserole it. She'd get the liver, flour and breadcrumb it, it wasn't as bad that way as it had the nice coating on it, but she'd cook it, then she'd turn it over and cook it some more, then she would overcook it some more. Then she'd stab it, and a bit of blood came out, so she'd cook it some more. Then she would take it out of the pan and leave it. Then obviously as it rests the juices come out, so what would she do? Put it back in. Basically she would cook it 'til there were no juices coming out of it. That way she was sure it was completely cooked, and we could eat it. Can you imagine trying to eat a bit of liver that way? It used to dry my mouth out, it used to make me ill. So then she used to hide it under the mash. Obviously I used to eat the other stuff and try and keep it hidden, but she'd find it. Sometimes we would have a stand-off. I would sit down to tea at 6 o'clock, and by 8 o'clock it was stone cold and I was still battling, I was not eating it. Just a bit more, just one little bit. Just eat that one little piece. As if you were a two-year-old. This went on into my teens. As a result of that, if anyone ever asked what food I didn't like, I would have said liver. Obviously now I would eat liver. I cook it and eat it and it's lovely. I did venison liver on a Gordon Ramsay programme, made the whole room eat it, and everyone was a bit scared of it, but it went down a storm. Fantastic! And I've done lamb's liver, roasted whole and sliced. Liver was my pet hate. Now it's actually really nice, if it's cooked properly.

Sometimes Mum would say it was my favourite, which was breast of lamb, rolled stuffed breast of lamb. That is something I do now. I've always used breast of lamb. When I opened The House for Richard Corrigan, I confited the breast of lamb, rolled it up, rubbed it with the confit cure, the garlic and the herbs, anchovy, and slow cooked it. We used to serve it with a bean cassoulet and put the lamb kidney on there with a rosemary skewer. Wonderful! Anchovy seasons it as it roasts but the garlic is the thing. It works great with beef too. I like anchovy pastes, like anchoide, a powerful thing. But they have to be good, because bad anchovies are horrible.

My Mum's a crap cook! Don't get me wrong, she taught me to cook, but she is fucking rubbish. But she did make an effort. I remember, my Dad was in business and he had this Chinese guy that he was doing stuff with. We used to get a lot of stuff from the docks, off the Chinese boats, and we used to go round his house. Chinese Tim and his wife Cathy. She used to make all these fried chicken wings and different things for us when we'd go round. I'd never had anything like that. We used to live on Chinese food in those days. And he'd take us to what used to be Chinatown. The original Chinatown was in Limehouse, by the docks. When I was a kid it had already moved to where it is now, but there were still some amazing Chinese restaurants left dotted around Limehouse. And because we went in there with a Chinaman we were alright, we used to get these flat curly noodle things I'd never seen, with steak cut on top, sirloin steak. Amazing stuff! I used to love special fried rice.

But I didn't get those little pink things, those little shrimps you got in it. They were a bit spooky. I loved the egg and the chicken and the pork. But the little shrimps, a bit weird. I was a very picky kid, yet I loved Chinese food. I loved beef, sweet and sour pork, chicken and rice, pancake rolls. When you were coming home from youth club you'd get a bag of chips, curry sauce, and a pancake roll. That was a big fried spring roll, with meat and bean shoots, they were nice. You had to be careful the grease didn't pour down your shirt.

I was a cry-y baby, I used to cry, always bored. This went on to my teens, when I used to bang my head against the wall. My Dad used to say for fuck's sake, go out and do something. There was nothing to do! I used to hate being indoors, everyone watching the Sunday afternoon film on TV. I used to go and put records on. That was all I cared about, listening to music. I think it must be a very instinctive thing, because I don't come from a musical family. I was always into music, I have memories of watching the Beatles on TV, all of that whole scene, Cilla Black, Burt Bacharach. I was so into music that my Mum gave me her teenage record collection, and a record player. So as a boy I had all my Mum's old 78s and I just used to play records all the time. Which is a shame, because 78s break as they were made of bakelite or whatever, and I'd always drop them. There were some gems in there like early Elvis, Bill Haley and the Comets, and originals that would be worth a fortune now. I grew up with that 60s rock and roll. I wasn't old enough to go and buy my own records at that point. So I was really reliant on what they had.

I used to get the hump, really, really bored. I was probably slightly pre-pubescent still, when my Mum said, "Go and make a cake." It's a bit of a cliché, everybody starts cooking with their mum. But I didn't start cooking with my Mum because she was this home baker and wonderful cook or anything, it was just, "Oh for fuck's sake go and do something!"

We used to go round to my auntie's some Sundays, my Dad's brother's wife, and she had a Jimmy Young cookbook. Jimmy Young was the Radio 2 DJ, nothing I used to listen to, boring talking and rubbish. But people used to ring in and say, "What's the recipe today, Jim?" I remember hearing it as a kid. And they published cookbooks of old Jimmy Young's recipes. I think you had a different volume every year. My auntie had this old Jimmy Young cookbook. And she lent it to me. So my earliest recipe book memory is the Jimmy Young cookbook, making ginger brandy snaps out of there. Seeing that you could get a book, and look at a little bit of text, follow it, weigh stuff out and make something, you know, that was my introduction to cookbooks.

"When I was a bit older I was looking for a present for my Mum, and I bought her a Robert Carrier book. It was colourful and the food looked interesting. And once I'd bought it for her I started reading it myself and basically commandeered it. I had it in my bedroom and I used to keep it under my bed and read it. Which is really weird."

RT
RIER

YOU

he Third
mmy Young
ookb○○k

PES FROM THE BBC
JIMMY YOUNG SHOW

LICATIONS

if i think Back, i should have
taken myself to one side and
given myself a chat

"I made my Mum and Dad dinner, they were very polite about it, but you could tell they didn't like it."

I just remember it being some kind of chicken in wine sauce. I remember the wine being pale and insipid and the chicken being pale with flaccid skin. Not nice. They braved it.

And then later on when Mum was at work late on a Monday, it kind of became my job to cook the tea. It was usually just a fry-up to be honest. That's how it worked, you had Sunday roast, then on a Monday it would be the leftovers from that. So if you had veg, bubble and squeak would feature quite heavily. Which was fantastic, because everybody likes bubble and squeak.

In the 70s things were getting more exotic, that's when spag bol came along. I remember Mum doing something really exotic like gammon steak, with sweetcorn and pineapple. That became a favourite.

If someone asked me what things do I really remember, the things I really liked are obvious. Pie, mash and liquor, smoked haddock, streaky bacon, and cheese on toast with bacon on top is the ultimate, always with brown sauce. Kippers too, with a little vinegar on them. Can't have poncey white wine vinegar, but you've got to have vinegar, because when it runs into the butter, it's the acidity, it just cuts that richness. The fishy, smoky, buttery juices, with a bit of vinegar. To me that is it!

The first TV cooking show that I can remember was the Galloping Gourmet. Everyone used to watch that. I enjoyed the creating of the dish, and then seeing them sitting and eating it. But it was an awful programme. And I've often wondered, as cooking wasn't a big deal back then, why myself (I'm not putting myself in the same category as these people), Gary Rhodes, Marco Pierre White, are all within a year or six months of the same age. What was it that suddenly made people want to cook?

I don't know. Now, the next generation you could see quite clearly. They all used to come and work for me, they all wanted to be Gordon, or Marco. But what made Marco want to cook? What made everybody interested in cooking, boys especially, at that time?

I used to go to work with my Dad a lot, see different things, see things that you hadn't seen before. I remember the first kebab shop, called Kebab Machine, in Shepherd's Bush. I remember going in there and thinking it was brilliant. I had a thing about caffs from an early age. So much so that I got out of bed once, and went down Walthamstow market trying to get work. I was about ten years old. My Mum woke up wondering where the fuck I'd gone. I'd managed to get a job for a couple of quid pulling the stalls out, and then I got a job in the caff just pouring tea and buttering bread. I loved it. Even at school, rather than be in lessons we used to bunk off, play pinball and sit in there all day. We used to get our dinner money, and spend that on fags. In those days the school sweetshop used to sell single cigarettes, in sweetie jars for a penny. Bizarre, isn't it! Who was that aimed at? Selling them to school kids. I think I had my first cigarette at seven. I stopped in my 20s. Everything changes when you stop. Occasionally I get a craving, but you try not to.

SPICED-MACKEREL-KEBAB, AUBERGINE-CHUTNEY, TAHINI-SAUCE

Ingredients: serves 4

Chermoula
1/2 red onion, peeled and chopped
1 clove of garlic, peeled and crushed
zest and juice of 1/2 lemon
85g olive oil
10g ground coriander
10g ground cumin
7g sweet paprika
1/4 bunch fresh coriander,
    stalks and all
1/8 bunch flat leaf parsley
1/4 bunch mint
7g ras el hanout
2g cayenne pepper
5g salt

4 fresh mackerel fillets, pin boned

Aubergine chutney
50ml olive oil
1 aubergine, diced
2.5g ground cumin
2.5g ground coriander
2.5g turmeric powder
2.5g yellow mustard seeds
2.5g chilli powder
1 red chilli, finely diced
2.5g salt
30g sugar
75ml white wine vinegar
2 peeled cloves garlic, peeled
    and grated
2cm piece of ginger, grated

Tahini sauce
2.5g ground cumin
10g tahini paste
2.5g fine sea salt
50ml plain yoghurt
juice of 1/2 lemon

Flatbread
100g strong white flour
pinch of salt
5g fresh yeast
75ml tepid water
7g olive oil

fresh coriander, chopped

To make the chermoula, place all the ingredients in a food processor and blitz to a rough paste. Lay the mackerel fillets in a dish then pour the charmoula paste over the fish making sure they are all evenly coated. Chill them in the fridge until needed.

To make the aubergine chutney, in a non-reactive pan, heat the olive oil and fry the aubergine until golden. Depending on the size of your pan, you might want to do this bit in a couple of batches to make sure it fries rather than boils. Once browned, remove to a bowl. Add all the spices to the pan and fry for a minute before adding the salt, sugar and vinegar. Grate in the garlic and ginger, add the reserved aubergine, then give everything a stir to make sure it's all amalgamated. Reduce the heat then leave to simmer, until thick and chutney-like, giving it the occasional stir to make sure it doesn't catch on the bottom of the pan. Leave to cool.

To make the tahini sauce, whisk the cumin, tahini and salt into the yoghurt. Stir in the lemon juice to taste then chill it in the fridge.

To make the flatbread, put all the ingredients into a food mixer fitted with a dough hook and knead for a couple of minutes until smooth. Cover the bowl with cling film and leave to prove for about 30 minutes, or until doubled in size.

Warm a dry frying pan or griddle. Divide the bread dough into 4 golf-ball-size pieces, and on a floured surface roll the dough balls as thinly as possible. Bake them one at a time in the pan or griddle for 1 minute on each side until lightly browned and speckled.

To serve, heat your grill to its hottest setting. Grill the generously chermoula-coated fillets, skin side up, until charred and blistered. They should take about 2 or 3 minutes to cook depending how hot your grill gets. Spoon a mound of aubergine chutney onto each flatbread, top with a mackerel fillet, drizzle with the tahini and a scattering of chopped coriander then roll your kebabs into cone shapes. I think these are best eaten with your hands but feel free to use a knife and fork if you must.

AFTER CLOSING TIME AT OUR LOCAL PUB A COUPLE OF NEIGHBOURS USED TO BANG ON OUR DOOR, PISSED, WANTING A KEBAB. ONE DAY, I HAD SOME PITTA FROM OUR STAFF MEAL, MACKEREL, AUBERGINE AND SPICED CHERMOULA. AND WHEN THEY BANGED ON THE DOOR I GAVE IT TO THEM. THE NEXT DAY THEY CAME BACK, SOBER, AND SAID IT WAS THE BEST KEBAB THEY HAD EVER EATEN

MELON-AND-HAM-GAZPACHO

THIS IS A CHILLED SOUP. THE ORANGE JUICE WORKS WELL, AND
THE VINEGAR BRINGS A TOUCH OF ACIDITY. I USED TO SWIRL
OLIVE OIL INTO IT, BUT IF YOU FREEZE THE OLIVE OIL YOU CAN
DROP A CUBE ON TOP AND IT MELTS INTO THE SOUP

Ingredients: serves 6

2 ripe Charentais melons
125ml freshly squeezed orange juice
5g fine sea salt
freshly ground white pepper
10ml Moscatel vinegar
50ml of your favourite olive oil
50g Iberico ham, sliced
a small handful of nasturtium leaves

To make the soup, remove the seeds from the melons, scoop out the flesh and put into a blender. Blitz until smooth, add the orange juice and salt and pepper. Taste to check the seasoning before adding the vinegar - depending on the sweetness of the melons and orange juice, you may decide to add a little more or a little less. Put the soup in the fridge until well chilled.

Put the olive oil into a small ice cube tray and freeze.

Slice the ham into small strips.

To serve, pour the chilled soup into bowls and put an ice cube of olive oil in the middle. Garnish with the ham and nasturtium leaves.

TARAMASALATA

Ingredients: serves 8

Taramasalata
175g white sliced bread,
    crusts removed
150g smoked cods' roe
200g extra virgin olive oil
juice of 1 lemon

Pickled vegetables
150ml Moscatel vinegar
50ml water
5g fine sea salt
30g golden caster sugar
1 small cauliflower, separated
    into florets
1 banana shallot, peeled, sliced
    and separated into rings
2 carrots, peeled and sliced
1 Chioggia beetroot, peeled
    and thinly sliced

Croutons
50g butter
25ml olive oil
1 clove of garlic, peeled
    and crushed
1 stale baguette, sliced
    very thinly

a small handful of pea shoots

To make the taramasalata, soak the bread in cold water for a few seconds until completely wet. Using your hands, squeeze all the water out of the bread to form a soggy paste. Put the bread into a food processor. Peel the membrane from the roe and add to the bread. Whiz them to a smooth paste. Slowly add the oil and lemon juice. Transfer to a piping bag and chill it in the fridge until ready to serve.

To make the pickled vegetables, heat the vinegar, water, salt and sugar in a non-reactive pan, until dissolved. Leave to cool before pouring over the vegetables and chill it in the fridge until ready to serve.

To make the croutons, in a small saucepan, melt the butter with the oil and garlic. Brush the mixture all over the bread slices and bake them on a tray for around 10 minutes at 180°C, or until crisp and golden.

To serve, pipe a couple of little mounds of taramasalata onto each plate with the vegetables and croutons arranged around, and garnish with the pea shoots.

An addition of a few raw vegetables such as radishes or asparagus would make a nice contrast. You could also turn it into a more substantial salad by adding soft-boiled quail eggs. Be creative.

THIS IS A THROWBACK DINNER PARTY DISH. CRUDITES AND A DIP ON A PLATE. THE VEG CHOICES ARE UP TO YOU, IT DEPENDS WHAT TIME OF YEAR YOU'RE MAKING IT

LAMB-BACON, SWEETBREAD, PEAS

THiS DiSH iS A TAKE oN PETiT PoiS A la FRANçAiSE, PERFECT
FoR lAMB iN THE SPRiNG, AND A RiFF oN liVER AND BACoN.
i DiD lAMB BACoN AS PART oF A DiSH FoR GREAT BRiTiSH
MENu, AND iT'S SoMETHiNG i AlWAyS GET ASKED ABoUT

Ingredients: serves 6

2 trimmed, boneless breasts
   of lamb
500g duck or lamb fat

Cure
50g sea salt
40g golden caster sugar
10g sweet smoked paprika
4 sprigs of thyme

Sweetbreads
50g sea salt
500ml cold water
6 plump lamb sweetbreads

Pea cream
1 banana shallot, peeled and
   finely sliced
5g fine sea salt
200ml whipping cream
300g frozen peas
freshly ground white pepper

3 heads of baby gem lettuce
salt and pepper to taste
a handful of peas
6 small spring onions
a few pea shoots

To make the lamb bacon, trim the breasts of any excess fat. Mix all of the cure ingredients together and rub all over the lamb. Lay the breasts on top of each other, and then trim the ends to square them off. Cut them in half and lay each half on top of each other, creating a thick block. Vacuum pack or wrap tightly in cling film and leave to cure overnight.

Melt the duck or lamb fat in a pot just big enough to hold the lamb. Add the lamb, cover with a lid and then cook in an oven at 160°C for two-and-a-half hours, until completely tender. Leave to cool for about 30 minutes before carefully removing to a tray. Try to keep the breasts together in a block. Place another tray on top and then weigh it down with whatever you can find. Leave it in the fridge to press, until cold and set.

To make the sweetbreads, dissolve the salt in the water and soak the sweetbreads for 2 hours. Rinse in clean water for about an hour before removing all sinew and membrane. Dry on a cloth and chill them in the fridge until required.

To make the pea cream, sweat the shallots in a knob of butter, add the salt and cook for a few minutes or until completely soft. Add the cream and the peas. Bring to a boil and cook for about 3 minutes. Transfer everything to a blender, add a few grinds of pepper and blitz until completely smooth. Push through a fine sieve and then chill it in the fridge quickly, to retain the colour.

To serve, cut the lamb into thick rashers. Fry on each side to crisp (try to keep them in one piece). Remove from the pan and keep warm. Add another knob of butter and sauté the sweetbreads until golden. Keep them warm with the lamb while you fry the onions until charred and wilted.

Cut the lettuce in half lengthways, add another knob of butter then add the lettuce, cut side down and fry until coloured. Season with salt and pepper, add a splash of water and boil vigorously to soften. Blanch the peas, drain, then toss with a spoon of the pea cream. Place the rashers on your warm plates. Spoon or pipe on a little purée. Put a lettuce half on each plate, a spoonful of peas, an onion and a sweetbread and finish with a few pea shoots.

GINGER-CAKE

Ingredients: makes 1 cake, 8-12 slices depending on your appetite

170g butter
185g black treacle
170g golden syrup
225g dark soft brown sugar
450g plain flour
10g mixed spice
10g ground ginger
15g baking powder
5g bicarbonate of soda
5g fine sea salt
2 large free range eggs
550ml milk
100g stem ginger, drained finely chopped

To make the ginger cake, melt the butter, treacle, syrup and sugar in a pan, being careful not to burn.

Mix together the flour, spice, ground ginger, baking powder, bicarbonate of soda, and salt. Beat in the eggs, then the milk to make a smooth batter. Add the melted sugar mixture then fold in the stem ginger.

Pour into a lined and greased 24cm square baking tin, or a loaf tin, and bake at 180°C for about 45 minutes.

Leave to cool on a rack.

THIS REMINDS ME OF THE JAMAICA GINGER CAKE I LOVED AS A KID. I DEHYDRATE THIN SLICES OF THIS TO SERVE WITH FOIE GRAS. BUT EQUALLY EVERYBODY LIKES A PIECE OF CAKE WITH A CUP OF TEA. THIS GETS BETTER AND BETTER OVER THE FEW DAYS AFTER YOU MAKE IT

ALMOND-CAKE

Ingredients: makes 1 cake, 8-12 slices depending on your appetite

170g soft butter
170g golden caster sugar
3 large free range eggs, separated
85g self-raising flour
60ml Amaretto
85g ground almonds
5g fine sea salt

To make the cake, cream together the butter and sugar until very pale and fluffy. Beat in the egg yolks one at a time, followed by a couple of tablespoons of the flour. Add the Amaretto and then the almonds and salt. Fold in the remaining flour. Whisk the egg whites to soft peaks then fold into the cake mix.

Pour into a lined 24cm square baking tin and bake at 170°C for approximately 45 minutes.

Leave to cool on a rack.

THIS IS OUR GO-TO CAKE RECIPE. IT HAS BEEN USED IN EVERY DESSERT GOING. I DEVELOPED IT AT THE HOUSE. AS A PLAIN CAKE IT'S GREAT, BUT YOU CAN ALSO SOAK IT IN SYRUPS. MADE WITH A SWEET WINE LIKE SAUTERNES IT'S GREAT

BANANA-CAKE

Ingredients: makes 1 cake, 8-12 slices depending on your appetite

Toffee
100g golden caster sugar
25g butter
150ml double dream

Banana cake
125g butter
240g golden caster sugar
3 large free range eggs
400g over-ripe mashed banana
1 vanilla pod
240g plain flour
5g baking powder
5g bicarbonate of soda
5g fine sea salt

To make the toffee, heat the sugar in a pan until very dark but not burnt. Whisk in butter and then the cream and cook until smooth and sauce-like.

To make the banana cake, cream together the butter and sugar until very pale and fluffy. Beat in eggs one at a time followed by the banana and the seeds from the vanilla pod.

Fold in all the remaining dry ingredients then swirl in the toffee. Don't mix the toffee too much, swirls and streaks are good.

Pour into a lined 1kg loaf tin, or muffin moulds, and bake at 180°C for approximately 30 minutes or about 20 minutes if muffins.

Leave to cool on a rack.

THIS IS ACTUALLY A BANANA MUFFIN RECIPE, YOU CAN MAKE MUFFINS WITH IT, OR A LOAF OR CAKE. YOU WANT TRULY MANKY BANANAS FOR THIS, STRONG SMELLING AND BROWN. WHEN THEY'VE HAD IT IS WHEN THEY'VE GOT THEIR MOST INTENSE FLAVOUR

My DAD'S AuNTiE HAD A
PiE aND MASH SHOP

SCHOOLBOY

yes!

COME IN
WE ARE
OPEN

"Pie, mash and liquor is proper East End food. You couldn't go past a pie and mash shop without having it. There's not so many of them now, but I like to take people when I can. It's a new experience for them. People that are from West London or Dover or wherever, who've never had it, their usual response is, "I don't want any of that green stuff on my pie!"."

"It's parsley sauce, the liquor, made with eel stock, because they were pie and eel shops."

Nowadays I don't think you'd find anyone makes them with eel stock. It's generally parsley stock thickened with cornflour. People find it a bit weird, but when you're brought up on it, it's great. You've got to put loads of vinegar on it and loads of white pepper. It sounds disgusting that the pies are all soft with soggy bottoms to them and an almost burnt top, and the mash has no butter in it, it's just potato. The mince and the thin gravy run out of the pie, not like a thickened gooey pie. It's a puddingy thing, with the liquor, the gravy, the pastry, and then vinegar and white pepper. Eat it all together, and you can't go wrong.

I use white pepper all the time. Black pepper has a bitterness to it and a fragrance, which are all very nice in a salad or on a particular dish. If you are being all poncey, you want cracked black pepper. But we didn't eat that, we didn't have black pepper. In the pepper-shakers on the caff table, it was like dust. Back in those days we didn't know what black pepper was. Pepper's pepper, and it comes in dust form in a little shaker, same as the salt. There was no flaking a bit of Maldon on your pie and mash, be real! And the vinegar, I don't think it was even malt vinegar, I think it was 'non-brewed condiment'. You could probably strip the paint off your floor with that. They had it in old glass bottles, and they added some chillies, dried chillies obviously. I don't think I'd ever seen a fresh one. It gave this heat to the vinegar that's just great. When I was young I was scared of the chilli vinegar, purely because there were things in it. It had to be clear. Later I went through a phase of wanting to eat spicy food. So now if I go to a pie and mash shop, I always seek out the one bottle of chilli vinegar floating around the tables.

My friend Eddie was a real tearaway nightmare of a kid. He used to beat his sister up, and chase her down the street. We always knew he was completely out of order. I remember the sight of his Dad chasing after him. He could never catch him, and he would beat his sister senseless. The only way his Dad could ever get him to come home was to promise to buy him something. Don't beat your sister up; I'll buy you a bike. He had the ten-gear racing bike.

Eddie had a piano. It surprised me that he was musical, he could play beautifully. He could play really good classical piano. I didn't see how. It turned out he was going to piano lessons with a teacher called Mrs Hugget. We got a piano, so I could start to learn. And my Dad used to make me play chopsticks with him as our party trick when people came over. I had a really shitty old cheap acoustic guitar, with steel strings, and I wanted to learn to play it. Mrs Hugget taught guitar as well, albeit classical. So I went along with Eddie to meet her. I took my guitar, and she said, "Okay, show us what you know." She tried to teach me, but it took her only one lesson to tell me, "A; the guitar is shit and B; you ain't gonna be a guitar player, look at your fingers!" But I persevered. I got a better guitar for Christmas from Woolworths. It was an audition semi-acoustic, a copy of a Gibson 335, with its little amp. I still couldn't play it. That was when I was about 10 years old. Mrs Hugget basically put me off.

So then I started piano lessons with her. My Dad said that if I learnt to play Für Elise in a month he'd give me a tenner, or it might have been a fiver. I managed it up to the first movement. I can still remember a bit of it. But like all lessons it becomes like school. I hated anything academic. She was asking have you done any work, have you done any practice, have you done this, have you done that? I've had golf lessons, because I play golf now. I have a lesson and they ask, did you practise? What's the point of having a lesson? You can teach me anything, but once I leave, that's it, 'til the next time I come back. I'll come every week. I'll come three times a week. But I don't do practice, anything like that becomes a chore and it takes the enjoyment out of it.

I'd got this electric organ and I taught myself to play that. I used to play the solo from House of the Rising Sun. That was all I could play. My brother had a little band and they used to rehearse in his bedroom. I thought I could be their keyboard player. Luckily they did the House of the Rising Sun! But their drummer was shit, and he had a little strop one day when they were round our house. I'm sure it was over us having no baked beans in the house, or something ridiculous. I always remember: "What no beans?!" because my Mum had left them a bit of lunch. Anyway they had a big row and he stormed off. I sat at this drum kit and just started playing, and everybody looked up. They all said I could play better than the drummer. I'd never been on a drum kit in my life. He didn't know what he was doing, and I kind of knew which hand you use for the high hat, and that you play the off beats with the snare. Then you have the bass pedal in between, and you play four-four time. It was a bit stilted, but it was natural. So I became the drummer, instantly.

We had a gig, playing for the local newspaper event in the Lloyd Park Pavilion, Walthamstow. It was a local talent show, with loads of different acts, bands, singers, dancers, ballet and that. We headlined it doing two songs. One song was written by the singer, and was called Love and Black Death, suitably teenage. They were all about three years older than me. I was 11, they were 14-year-olds. I couldn't tell you what the band was called, we never had a name. I think we made one up on the spot. I think the guitarist turned round jokingly and said something like Red Rabbit, and that's what was in the paper. That was my first live appearance.

This was pre-punk. That whole notion that punk gave people the attitude to think, I can do that; well I think if you wanted to do it you just did it anyhow.

Then Dad got us some gigs in the Telegraph pub in Plaistow, on Wednesday nights. It was the kind of place where blokes came in with sawn-offs. I was drumming, my brother was playing guitar. The landlord there let us play. We didn't get paid but we got free drinks. I always used to drink light and bitter in those days. The reason I used to drink light and bitter was they used to give you your glass with half a pint of bitter in it, which more often than not was three quarters of a pint, they never measured like now, and then you'd get your bottle of light ale. So you'd get much more than a pint. I was 11. I used to get three light and bitters a night.

We could try out songs, and the songwriter, the guitarist/singer, used to write a lot of stuff. The rest was all covers. I wasn't very aware of some of the music we were playing then, I hadn't discovered it yet. But we were playing things like early Pink Floyd. As far as I was concerned he could have written them. This was the 70s, and we were doing stuff like JJ Cale, Eric Clapton, and early Fleetwood Mac. I learnt those through playing them. It wasn't really for me, but it was a good grounding. I always remember him taking me to see a band in West Kensington, at the Nashville, which was quite a famous music venue. We went to see a band from Australia, a young band, who had just come out, called AC/DC. And the support band were called Last Exit, with a bass player who wore a stripy rugby shirt. That was Sting.

At that time I had a Saturday job at the butcher's. That was a bit of an eye opener. I used to make the sausages, which was my main job on a Saturday. They used to have two bins, one of seasoning and one of rusk, a big mincer and a big bowl chopper. I'd mince the meat, put it in a bowl chopper, chuck it all round, put water in it, a scoop of rusk, and seasoning. That's your sausagemeat. Then you put it in the machine and make sausages. And every Saturday we would have a break, and eat some. They'd make rolls. They also used to do things like tongue rolls and black pudding rolls. Now as a fussy kid and a fussy eater, you're not going to eat that, are you?

During my school days, when I was 12 or 13, I very rarely had lunch in school. We used to get our dinner money and spend it on fags. So the way to survive, because you've spent your money on fags, would be to go to the bakers, and they'd give you yesterday's stale cakes or bread for a penny. You'd buy stale bread, pull the stale crumb out of the middle, go to the chippy, and either buy tuppence-worth of chips, which is a big bag, or ask if they'd got any scraps. If they had any they'd give you the scraps of batter out of the fryer, they're free, and there's always chips in amongst them. You put that into your bread, and add loads of salt and vinegar. There's major nutrition in that!

Or you'd go to the pie shop, and you couldn't afford the pie so you'd have a bowl of mash and liquor. They'd give you a bowl, a couple of scoops of mash, a dollop of liquor and you'd put vinegar on it. Occasionally the lady would take pity and give you a pie. So for 2p, you'd get pie, mash and liquor. That was dinner, and your fags, and a beer sometimes.

PICKLED-ONIONS

Ingredients: makes 3 x 500g jars

300g sea salt
1500ml water
1 kilo of cipollini onions, peeled

Pickle
750ml white wine vinegar
500ml water
375g golden caster sugar
1 tbsp yellow mustard seeds
1 tsp black peppercorns
1 tsp caraway seeds
1 large sprig of thyme
1 bay leaf

Dissolve the salt in the water and pour over your peeled onions. Put a plate or saucepan lid directly on top to help keep them submerged, then chill them in the fridge for a week.

To make the pickle, in a non-reactive pan, bring all the ingredients to the boil.

Wash the onions thoroughly then add to the simmering pickle liquor.

Remove them from heat and leave to cool.

Store in sterilised jars.

They'll be ready in a month.

WHAT COULD BE MORE BRITISH THAN A PICKLED ONION?
I GET PEOPLE EATING THE WHOLE JAR, AND HAVE
COUNTLESS REQUESTS TO TAKE A JAR HOME

SAUSAGE-ROLLS

NICE IN ITS SIMPLICITY. THE RECIPE ISN'T WRITTEN IN STONE,
YOU COULD MAKE YOUR OWN SAUSAGEMEAT OR BUY YOUR
FAVOURITE FROM YOUR BUTCHER'S, AND YOU DON'T HAVE
TO INCLUDE FOIE GRAS

Ingredients: serves 8

Filling
1 banana shallot, peeled and
    finely chopped
1kg of your favourite pork
    sausagemeat
100g diced foie gras, optional
1 small black truffle (tinned is fine)

Rough puff pastry
225g plain flour
3g fine sea salt
300g chilled butter
iced water

To make the filling, sweat the shallot in a little vegetable oil until soft, then mix into all the other filling ingredients. Using a large sheet of cling film form the mixture into a long sausage shape. Chill it in the fridge until ready to use.

To make the rough puff pastry, put the flour, salt and butter into a food processor and roughly pulse. Make sure you don't turn it into a fine breadcrumb-type mix, you want big lumps of butter. Add just enough water to just bring it together, the pastry should be fairly dry. Flatten your dough and shape into a rough rectangle and chill it in the fridge for a few minutes to firm up.

Roll the pastry into a rectangle a couple of centimetres thick. Fold the top third down to the centre, then the bottom third up and over that. Give the dough a quarter turn (to the left or right) and roll it out again to three times the length. Fold as before, and cover with cling film. You can now store it in the fridge or freezer until required.

Roll out your pastry to a thickness of about 5mm. Trim to create a straight edge. Unwrap your sausage and place on the pastry along the straight edge. Roll over in the pastry and cut along the length of the sausage roll. Place on a parchment-lined baking tray then brush with egg yolk.

Bake at 200°C for 20 minutes.

For an extra glaze and flavour boost, while still warm brush with an equal mix of black treacle and Marmite.

Using a serrated knife, slice into sausage rolls of whatever size you fancy.

We serve these with Madeira sauce at The West House, but they're great with your favourite gravy or with a dollop of HP sauce.

BLACK-PUDDING

Ingredients: makes 3 sausages,
20 slices depending on your
appetite

1 litre fresh pig's blood
1 tsp white wine vinegar
120g onion, peeled and finely diced
120g leek, finely diced
120g streaky bacon, finely diced
a little vegetable oil
3 cloves of garlic, peeled and grated
80g pinhead oatmeal
1/4 bunch of fresh marjoram,
    picked and chopped
5 sprigs thyme, picked and
    chopped
1/4 nutmeg, grated
1tsp allspice berries, ground
1tsp white peppercorns,
    freshly ground
2tsp fine sea salt
20g lardo, diced

To make the black pudding, using a blender, blitz the blood with the vinegar to stop it from clotting.

Sweat the onion and leek in a little vegetable oil until soft and translucent. Add the bacon and continue to sweat for a few minutes until the bacon is cooked. Add the garlic and oatmeal. Continue to cook to a thick porridge.

In a separate saucepan, gently warm the blood, stirring all the time until it starts to thicken and change to a dark brown colour. This should happen at around 80°C. Gradually stir the blood into the porridge mixture. Add the herbs and seasonings. Finally stir in the diced lardo, making sure it's evenly distributed through the mixture.

Spread into a cling film-lined baking tray or loaf tin. Bake in a bain-marie in a low to moderate oven for about 1 hour or until firm to the touch. Chill it in the fridge and then remove from the tin.

Alternatively use cling film to shape into sausages. Wrap each sausage tightly in foil then gently poach for about 30 minutes, or until firm. Chill it in the fridge before unwrapping.

To serve, cut into whatever shapes you fancy, or slice into rounds if using sausages. Fry both sides in a little oil and butter until warm and crisp.

YOU REALLY NEED TO USE FRESH BLOOD, IF YOU CAN GET IT,
IT DOESN'T WORK THE SAME WITH DRIED.
THE RECIPE SAYS BAKE IT IN A TRAY, BUT YOU COULD
PUT IT IN CASINGS, BAKE IT IN DIFFERENT TINS,
OR ROLL IT IN CLING FILM AND POACH LIKE A SAUSAGE

ECCLES-CAKES

I DON'T WANT TO OFFEND ANYONE FROM ECCLES IN DARING TO
PROPOSE A RECIPE, I'M NOT A NORTHERNER. THESE ARE
PREDOMINANTLY CURRANTS, AS THEY SHOULD BE, BUT THEY
ARE NOT STRICTLY AUTHENTIC. WE LIKE THEM

Ingredients: serves 8

Filling
75g butter
75g soft light brown sugar
zest of an orange
5g ground cinnamon
3g grated nutmeg
75g currants
75g golden raisins
50g chopped mixed peel

Rough puff pastry
225g plain flour
3g fine sea salt
300g chilled butter
iced water
1 egg, beaten
sprinkling of caster sugar

To make the filling, melt the butter and sugar together and carry on cooking gently until it turns a deep golden colour. Add the orange zest, cinnamon and nutmeg. Cook for a couple of minutes then add the fruit and mixed peel.

Stir everything together and keep cooking until you have a thick sticky mix. Remove from the pan and leave to cool.

To make the rough puff pastry, put the flour, salt and butter into a food processor and roughly pulse. Make sure you don't turn it into a fine breadcrumb-type mix, you want big lumps of butter. Add just enough water to just bring it together, the pastry should be fairly dry. Flatten your dough and shape into a rough rectangle and chill it in the fridge for a few minutes to firm up.

Roll the pastry into a rectangle a couple of centimetres thick. Fold the top third down to the centre, then the bottom third up and over that. Give the dough a quarter turn (to the left or right) and roll it out again to three times the length. Fold as before, and cover with cling film. You can now store it in the fridge or freezer until required.

Roll out your pastry to a thickness of about 3mm. Using a pastry cutter, cut out 8 discs. Place a ball of the cooled filling in the centre of each pastry. Pull the edges up to make a ball shape and squash all the edges together to seal.

Place them on a lined baking tray, making sure the rough side is on the bottom. Brush with beaten egg, and sprinkle lightly with caster sugar. Put three slashes in each.

Bake at 200°C for 20 minutes.

Leave to cool on a wire rack.

SCHOOL'S-OUT FOREVER

i HATED school with a Passion

"I wasn't bad at learning, I was in the top group in everything. But I was very lazy, there was always something else to do."

The girls' school was down the road and the only time there were any mixed classes was languages. Hence taking every language possible. I took Spanish and German, and you had to take French. I was really into languages, but I never learnt anything. It just meant that I could hang out with girls.

When we had a careers talk I said I wanted to be a rock star. And that was punishable, you know, detention. I was always on fucking detention. You could save up your detention, three detentions and trade it for a cane. It bloody hurt, they used to make you bleed. Some of those teachers were sadistic.

I got to the point where I thought, "Right, I can't do this anymore." I thought the best way round it was not to turn up at the beginning of term when they mark the register. Whenever you started a new class, they did a register and there was always a kid's name there that had moved or something, some kid that didn't exist. This kid's name would get called out three or four times and everyone would yell back that he wasn't there, that he had never been there. And in the end it was struck off and you'd never hear of him again. So what I decided to do was not turn up at the very first day of school, registration, to see what happened. And true enough, guess what? Nothing happened, I just stopped going to school. But one day a school report arrived and on every page it said, "Who is this boy?"

I stayed out of school until I got caught. But then when I was 15 my National Insurance card came through the post, it was a good four or five months before I was 16. As soon as I had got that NI card, with a National Insurance number, having worked all my life, done everything to get jobs, I could legitimately get a job. So I just quit school.

They said I couldn't leave. I walked out of the school gates, went to get a bus, and waved back at them from the bus stop outside.

My first legitimate job was as a butcher at Sainsbury's, putting frozen chickens on the counter. It was supposed to be butchery but they didn't actually do any. I wanted to cook but that was a no-no for my Dad. There was a guy he knew from the pub, he seemed to be doing well, selling meat in there that he'd stolen. The joke was that he was building his own cow because he had a different bit of animal down his coat every time he came in the pub. He said he could get me a job in the slaughterhouse, so Dad and I went for a recce. It was a Jewish slaughterhouse, so there were rabbis there doing their thing. It's kind of evil, watching them slit the animal's throats and bleed them. Dad went green. It wasn't for me, but that is where butchery starts.

I answered an advert for a trainee butcher at Jones's in Chingford. They were really old-school, old boys that did everything, and that's where my learning really started. There was one of the old boys, Jack, who gave me all of his old books from his apprenticeship, books from Smithfield. You used to go to Smithfield to college to learn butchery properly.

I learned how to break down a carcass. I learned how to put that into joints, how to tie meat, how to prepare the fat, the relevance of having the fat on the meat, the differences between a forequarter of beef as opposed to the hindquarter of beef, and what it entails. There's ways for a butcher, in the way they cut, to add an extra bone or a half to the piece that's a bit more expensive to sell.

You wouldn't think it would be relevant to you as a chef, you just want a prime bit. But it is. As a chef you have to make money and it's good to know the ins and outs of butchery skills and practice.

They used to do all their own salt beef, silversides and salt pork, tongues and corned beef. They'd put it in brine, and pickle it. I didn't know what any of that was before that. And again, sausages, but we were making sausages with different meats, and I was learning why you put bread in, why you put water in, what it does, how it changes it. They took the effort to tell me and to explain, even though it was at a very basic level.

Those old boys taught me loads.

I met Fred Ball through a friend of my Mum, someone she used to work with. Fred's sister was older than him, and she babysat for us. Sometimes we'd be left round their house. His mum was a singer in pubs and clubs. His granddad used to play banjo. Fred sang. They were a very musical family, which was great for me. I stayed in touch with Fred as we got older, purely because we shared an interest in music. Later on he was a drummer, playing in bands. I used to go along with him and started roadie-ing for him, although Pete Webb, their usual bass player, did moan about me being there. "Do we always have to have this fucking little kid hanging around us." Fred was a bit of a mentor for me in the old drumming thing, but at the time I was there because I was his roadie. I met Phil Collen with him, Fred introduced me to Phil. In around '78, they formed The Original Dumb Blondes. It was Fred and Phil, they brought in Jeff Hepting to be the singer and Pete on bass.

So I became the roadie for The Original Dumb Blondes. There was a point in their set, Fred being Fred, when he used to do this little cabaret in a feather boa.

It was a bit of comedy, a bit of fun and he used to get up and sing. So I used to get up and play drums for that slot. Fred had a pain-in-the-arse girlfriend who he was always rowing with, which made him late for rehearsals. Then they had a big fallout one day because of his girlfriend, everyone was really fed up with it. Phil had had enough so he left, and the band split up. Me and Phil went off and auditioned for Girl, which he joined but I didn't. He forced me into other auditions. We'd go to watch bands together. I had no confidence, but he used to say, "Well you're better than him, you're better than that guy tonight."

All this time, around '78, '79, I was working in the butcher's shop. But I would be coming home from The Music Machine, which was a great club, after watching Japan or whoever. Japan are why The Dumb Blondes existed! The place shut at two in the morning, so you can imagine what time I got home. I'd go to work and I'd just be shot to bits.

During that time, after Phil joined Girl, Pete and Jeff decided to reform, but instead of it being The Original Dumb Blondes, it got shortened to just Dumb Blondes. It was more in tune with what was happening, with New Romantic stuff coming up. It was more of a rock band before with Phil, who went on to join Def Leppard. So we then formed as a band with me as a drummer, Jeff singing, Pete on bass and we auditioned and got a keyboard player in, and a new guitarist, God bless him. I felt sorry for him because he was stepping into Phil's shoes. He was never going to be good enough.

"So Dumb Blondes were born, and we were getting more serious and working harder. While I was trying to work in the butcher's and be up all night. That's when the whole thing came to a head. I was out gigging at night and then into work the next day. I'd have accidents and cut my fingers and hands, cutting myself to ribbons. Then I'd play a gig the next night with stitches in, and as I'd hit the cymbal I'd catch my hand."

YBOARDS) GRAHAM (DRUMS) PETE (B

BLOOD WAS FLYING ALL OVER
ALL THE FRONT ROW

Then I would go to work next day and stab myself again. Once I was boning out a hindquarter of beef with a boning knife, and I slipped. I was probably a bit tired. I stabbed myself at the top of my leg, and it stuck in quite badly. I was in shock and came out of the cutting shed with the knife sticking out of me, and ran up through the back door and into to the shop. Everyone looked at me, there was a customer, an old lady, and there was blood pumping everywhere. "I've stabbed myself in the fucking bollocks!" I couldn't look down. They looked at it. Luckily, although your femoral artery is there, I missed it, but only just. I went to hospital, and they patched me up, as they had my hands many times. Next I crushed my hand putting a lamb up on a hook. It fell off, rock-hard out of the freezer. I missed the hook and it came down, and smashed against a marble slab. My finger just exploded. It's still all scarred and squashed there. I just thought, "This is really not the job to be doing if I want to be a musician."

Then my Nan died of cancer. I was a bit of a mess at work because I hadn't been to bed all night. I went to work the next day and was upset. The boss said to me, "Look, why don't you go home? Why don't you take a week, or two, sort yourself out and then when you come back get your hair cut." I had long hair, so I couldn't go in the shop. He said, "Cut your hair and smarten yourself up, maybe put a tie on and we'll move you on up into the shop."

I went home, the funeral was a few days later, and I felt I didn't want to go back. So I didn't and it was as simple as that. I made my mind up while I was off, and I spoke to my parents about it and they said, "Okay, you can have a year and live here rent-free and then we'll review the situation."

Suddenly I started getting stuff done. That's when we then got our first record deal and things started happening, because I was out there hustling myself.

FRIED-PIG'S-HEAD

THIS IS A TAKE ON VEAL HOLSTEIN, AN ESCALOPE,
BREADCRUMBED AND FRIED, TOPPED WITH EGG,
ANCHOVIES AND BEURRE NOISETTE

Ingredients: serves 6

Fried pig's head
half pig's head
1 onion, peeled and chopped
2 carrots, peeled and sliced
1 stick of celery, sliced
1 large sprig of thyme
1 bay leaf
3 cloves garlic, peeled and crushed
5g fine sea salt
freshly ground white pepper
fresh curly parsley, chopped

100g plain flour
9 large free range eggs
300g panko breadcrumbs
12 boquerones (marinated
    white anchovies), slivered
15g capers in salt, soaked to
    remove salt
2 piquillo peppers, cut into strips
12 cornichons, cut in half
    lengthways

To make the fried pig's head, using a blow lamp, singe any hairs from the head, paying special attention to the eyelashes and insides of the ears.

Place the head in a large saucepan, along with the vegetables, herbs and garlic. Cover with cold water. Add 2 tablespoons of salt.

Bring to the boil. Reduce the heat and continue to simmer for about 3 hours or until the head is very soft and tender. Leave in the pot until cool enough to handle.

Once cool, pick the head apart, saving all the skin, fat and meaty bits, whilst discarding bones, nerves, glands and anything that looks dodgy (you can save the ears for another day).

Chop the meat, cooked carrots and garlic from the pan quite finely, and mix together. Season with fine sea salt, and loads of fresh white pepper. Add a generous amount of chopped parsley.

Using a large pastry cutter, form the mixture into six firm patties. Chill them in the fridge to set.

Set up three containers, one for flour, one for 3 of the eggs, beaten, and one for panko. Start coating your patties by first dusting them in the flour, followed by the egg and finally the panko. Make sure they are well coated.

To serve, gently fry the pig's head patties in a little oil and butter until golden brown on both sides. Do this slowly over a low heat so they turn nicely crisp and golden and heat all the way through. You could put them in a hot oven for a few minutes to heat through if you prefer.

Fry 6 eggs how you like them then place one on top of each patty. Garnish with the anchovies, capers, peppers and cornichons.

STREAKY-BACON

Ingredients: serves 6

Cure
250g coarse sea salt
1 tsp saltpetre, optional
50g soft brown or
    muscovado sugar
4 bay leaves
20g of thyme
1 tbsp black peppercorns,
    lightly crushed

1 large piece of fatty pork belly,
    roughly 2 kilos, on the bone

To make the cure, mix all the ingredients together in a bowl.

Place the pork belly in a container just big enough to hold it reasonably snugly and rub the cure all over.

Cover and chill it in the fridge for between five and seven days, turning occasionally.

Wash off all the cure residue and pat dry with a clean cloth.

Hang in the fridge or lay on a rack in the fridge, making sure there is plenty of air around the pork. Leave to dry for two weeks before removing the bones and slicing as required.

FOR BACON YOU NEED A GREAT PIECE OF PORK, AND SALT. YOU CAN VARY THE CURE, THE SUGARS, HERBS, AROMATS, AND WHETHER OR NOT YOU USE TREACLE. DEVELOP YOUR OWN CURE THE WAY YOU LIKE IT

THIS IS BETTER WITH LARGE TAME FRENCH RABBITS THAN THE
WILD ONES, WHICH ARE LEANER, TOUGHER AND HARDER TO COOK.
IN THE RESTAURANT I HAVE SERVED THIS WITH SPANISH
CROQUETAS, WHICH GO REALLY WELL. SEE HAKE DISH, PAGE 200

Ingredients: serves 4

1 large French farmed rabbit,
 separated into saddle, legs and
 forequarters

Stuffing
the legs from the rabbit
5g fine sea salt
100ml whipping cream
a few leaves of wild garlic or spinach
liver and kidneys from the rabbit,
 optional
freshly ground white pepper

Chorizo crust
150g raw cooking chorizo

Cure
zest of an orange
10 crushed black peppercorns
100g coarse sea salt
80g golden caster sugar
1 bay leaf
4 sprigs of thyme
2 cloves of garlic, peeled
 and crushed

Rillettes
the forequarters from the rabbit
250g duck fat
salt and pepper to taste

Pepper ketchup
30g golden caster sugar
30ml Forum Cabernet
 Sauvignon vinegar
1 jar of piquillo peppers

1 bunch of asparagus, trimmed
 and peeled

Bone and trim the rabbit saddle, without cutting all the way through the back.

To make the stuffing, remove the meat from the legs, cut into smallish pieces, put in a blender with the salt, and blitz to a purée. Put the blender jug and rabbit in the freezer for a few minutes to chill down. Add half the cream and blitz until smooth. Be careful not to split the mix. Chill it again, add a little pepper and then rub the mousse through a sieve. Put the mousse into a cold bowl. Chill it again then beat in the remaining cold cream by hand.

Blanch and refresh the wild garlic or spinach leaves. Squeeze all the water out and spread on a clean cloth to dry.

Very briefly sauté the rabbit offal (if using) in a little vegetable oil. Leave to cool. Season the rabbit loin and lay the leaves along the inside. Spread the mousse over the leaves (you may not need it all). Slice the liver and kidney and place on top of the mousse. Roll the saddle neatly, encasing all the stuffing, wrap tightly in cling film. Chill it in the fridge for 1 hour.

To make the crust, remove the chorizo skins. Whiz in a food processor to break down any big fibrous bits, then use a rolling pin to roll between two sheets of parchment to about 3mm thick. Remove the cling film from the saddle. Peel the top sheet of paper from the chorizo and lay the saddle on top. Trim the edges of the chorizo to the same length, then roll up, peeling the paper as you go. Wrap the whole thing very tightly in several layers of cling film and tie the ends.

To make the rillettes, blitz the cure ingredients together; rub over the forequarters. Cover and put in the fridge for 12 hours. Wash off under cold water, place in a small casserole with the duck fat. Cook in a low oven, 140°C, for 2 hours. Leave to cool, then pick all the meat from the bones. Stir in 2 tablespoons of fat and cooking juices. Check seasoning, and then using cling film roll tightly into a sausage shape. Put in the fridge to set.

To make the ketchup, heat the sugar and vinegar in a small non-reactive pan, until almost a caramel. Stir in the peppers and cook for a couple of minutes. Transfer to a blender, and purée until smooth. Push the purée through a sieve. Store in a squeezy bottle.

To serve, bring a pan of water to 60°C and poach the saddle, still in its cling film, for 25 minutes. Remove from water and unwrap. Gently dry with kitchen paper, before carefully frying in a pan with a little vegetable oil to crisp the chorizo. Boil the asparagus in salted water for 2 minutes. Slice the rillettes into rounds. Carve the saddle into 4 slices; stand 1 piece on each warmed plate. Pipe a few blobs of ketchup around. Place a piece of rillette on each plate with a couple of asparagus spears.

This works really well with gnocchi, see page 264.

ROAST-SUCKLING-PIG, BAKED-APPLE, BLACK-PUDDING

Ingredients: serves 4

1 suckling pig shoulder
fine sea salt
1 large onion, peeled and
   cut in half
1 carrot, peeled and thinly sliced
20g of thyme
2 bay leaves
1 star anise
8 black peppercorns
1/2 bottle dry white wine

Baked apples

4 small Cox's orange pippins
25g butter, melted
20g golden caster sugar
fine sea salt
4 slices of black pudding
freshly ground white pepper

Sauce

125ml Calvados
350ml brown chicken stock
salt and pepper to taste

Score the rind of the shoulder all over with the tip of a sharp knife. Massage the salt into the scored skin. Leave it uncovered in the fridge overnight to dry out. Put the vegetables, herbs, spices and wine into a roasting tin or casserole, just big enough to hold the pork. Roast in the oven for 25 minutes at 200°C. Turn down to 140°C and continue roasting for another hour-and-a-half to 2 hours. Leave to rest uncovered for 30 minutes.

To make the baked apples, slice the tops and bottoms off the apples. Score a line all the way around the middle of each apple. This should stop them from bursting in the oven. Brush the apples all over with melted butter and then roll them in the sugar. Place them on a tray, season and bake them for 12 minutes at 180°C, or until just soft. Fry the slices of black pudding in a knob of butter until crisp, before placing one on top of each apple.

To make the sauce, remove any excess fat from the pork roasting tray. Deglaze the tray with the Calvados, making sure you scrape up all the caramelised bits from the bottom of the tray. Add the stock and continue to boil until reduced to a syrupy consistency. Taste for seasoning before passing through a fine sieve.

To serve, put the shoulder on a carving board with the apples, a jug of sauce and some creamy buttery mashed potato or a big bowl of roast spuds.

I'VE USED THE SHOULDER HERE, FAMILY-STYLE,
AS FOR A SUNDAY ROAST lunch. IT'S NICE THAT AT
HOME YOU CAN DO IT THAT WAY. IF YOUR OVEN IS
BIG ENOUGH YOU COULD DO THE WHOLE PIG

FULL-TIME
MUSIC

AT THAT TiME i STARTED
TO call MySELF A MUSiCiAN,
i MADE SURE THAT i
WORKED EVERy DAy

"We did as many gigs as we could and we rehearsed. We were very fussy, though, we wouldn't do the pub circuit."

We always put ourselves a little bit above the pub circuit. I didn't want a support slot at the Bridge House or the Hope and Anchor. If you're playing on a little flat stage in the pub, you're all on the same level. Being the drummer, you can't be seen, and barely heard. So I wouldn't play unless I had a drum riser and a big PA.

So we were very selective of gigs, we could have done a lot more, but we built up our own little circuit of headline gigs in good places, like the Marquee. And we were doing a few supports in bigger places like the Lyceum.

We got a little record deal, with a company called Fresh Records, an indie label. We did a single, a double A-side produced by friends of ours, Pete and Buffin, who had been the bass player and the drummer from Mott The Hoople. They were a massive 70s band, very influential. Their biggest hit was All The Young Dudes, which was written by David Bowie and had him singing on it.

I got to know them when they started coming to our gigs. We used to sleep round Pete's house. He had a big house in Acton and everyone used to go back and sleep on the floor. Adam Ant used to sleep there, Captain Sensible and Dave Vanian from The Damned, there was a whole group of people who used to hang around and stay at this house. So I basically moved in.

They produced our first double A-side single, for Fresh Records. I used to hang around the BBC and Top of the Pops every week. All the DJs knew us, and our single got played on the radio a lot. Mike Reid used to play it, one side one night, and the other side the next night. I remember driving on the West Way and seeing him going home from White City.

He pulled up to chat to us out the window. So we were known to people like him and Richard Skinner and Tommy Vance, and we thought we were on our way!

A few of us went out to France, to this big music trade show that's on every January in Cannes, called Midem. All the music publishers go, to meet and greet, and we went out with Fresh Records.

They got us a little place to stay and we drove over. My brother and the keyboard player Andy actually did the driving. Me and Jeff the singer sat in the back. It's the most tedious fucking drive. I had the Adam and the Ants album that had just come out. I wasn't particularly into Adam and the Ants but it intrigued me. We drove for 24 hours non-stop with me and Jeff in the back banging on the front seats. Can you imagine, they were going insane, taking turns, one would sleep and the other one would drive, and we were yodelling away in the back and banging.

But when we got down there we had a great time.

We got taken to a club one night to see James Brown, but I was so bored. I didn't have patience for anything. I wasn't particularly into that kind of music at the time or that whole theatre of him collapsing and sweating and putting a cloak on and standing up and walking off, then him shaking it off and coming back again. I must be one of the only people ever to walk out of a James Brown concert, but I just couldn't take it. At the time I was into bands like Japan. And before that, Led Zeppelin and Deep Purple.

We went to another gig, a band that Fresh Records were looking after. It was the new band from Wilko Johnson, who had been the guitarist of Dr Feelgood. I'd loved Dr Feelgood in the early days. Afterwards we went to a club and met up with a band called The Q-Tips, whose singer was Paul Young. I don't remember much of the gig or the nightclub, because we were drinking a lot.

I do remember us running over cars, The Q-Tips started it! That was my first run-in with the police in another country.

So we had a bit of a mad time there. When it came time to go home, being the child that I was with no patience for anything (I was 18 but probably mentally still 14), I just didn't think I could cope with that journey, I couldn't sit in that car again. So they all went back in the car without me. The record company owner was persuaded it would be a good idea for me to stay on for a bit longer and he bought me a ticket home. A first class ticket home from Monte Carlo! But I had never travelled on my own. I got on the plane and sat up the front, and we made it to Paris, I mean it's not exactly far, is it? But we were fog-bound in Paris and had to stay in Paris overnight. The airport cleared, until there was almost no one around except me. I had a first class ticket, I would have been put in a hotel, wouldn't I? But I didn't know that. I didn't have a penny, so I slept in the airport lounge, on the seats. The French people took no notice of me, and I didn't talk to them because I didn't know what to say.

There was one young girl there who was hanging around, and she talked to me. We got some food together, and curled up on a bench. She looked after me in the airport until I got on a plane the next day.

I went straight from the airport to The Bridge House in Canning Town to see my mates the Ian Mitchell Band play. I met Jackie there. She claims that's the night we met. I remember turning up there in the dressing room, and everyone just taking the piss out of me because I'd been stuck in Paris in the fog.

I've never really forgiven the French or Air France for just leaving me in the airport. And I had a first class ticket. They weren't really interested, I was only an 18-year-old kid.

"We used to play quite a lot at the Moonlight Club in West Hampstead, quite a pivotal thing for us because it was a good little club. We built up a huge following there, we used to fill it out. We had some great bands support us there that went on to do big stuff, like Depeche Mode. And the guy who ran the place had another club up upstairs called the Starlight."

HE liKED US, AND HE GAVE
ME A ROOM TO STAY

> "I started doing a few shifts behind the bar of a lunchtime. And he wanted to manage the band."

He wasn't really a band manager but he helped us get gigs and he financed a little bit of this, that and the other. So the single was doing all right. And I pushed people I knew and hassled to get on this Gary Glitter tour.

The opening night was the Odeon in Taunton. We played all over the country and finished in London at the Dominion Theatre on Gary's birthday. It was supposed to be his 30th, but I think he was 30 every year! Gary Glitter, eh.... you'd have had no idea.

We were doing the tour, and also fitting in some of our own dates in between, in little clubs. We'd do the main gig, and just park our bus in the car park, in the middle of the town or wherever. When we went to Cambridge we lived in that car park for three days. But living in a tour bus we weren't eating properly. We thought we'd look after ourselves. So we bought crates of Lucozade and vitamin pills, Sanatogen. That's all we lived on and we got gradually sicker and sicker. Dave, the tour manager who was driving the bus, was just popping these vitamin pills like there was no tomorrow. So we changed his vitamin pills to laxatives for a laugh. He went missing in Newcastle. We couldn't find him anywhere. In the end we found him in the toilets locked in the cubicle. We couldn't get him out, or get a response, so we kicked the door down. He wasn't on the toilet, he was on the floor squatting against the wall, his head in his hands in pain. He was in such a state! He'd had about two weeks of laxatives every day without food. He was totally shot. It was horrible!

The guitar player was from Sunderland, so when we were in Sunderland we stayed at his parents. But I don't remember it. I was so ill. Then we played in Leicester, I think it was De Montford Hall.

The whole band stayed with my then girlfriend's parents, who put us up and ended up nursing me. I was really rough, although I tried to do the gig. When we got to Glasgow I collapsed. I had to cancel the show, and they put me in a hotel. I'm pretty sure Glitter paid for my hotel because we couldn't have afforded it. I was in quite a nice room, I remember laying in bed and suddenly feeling better, just because I was in a bed and watching the TV. It was some celebration of Coronation Street having been on forever, all these black and white reruns of the original Coronation Street with Ena Sharples in a hairnet. Lying there ill in a hotel in Glasgow watching black and white reruns of Coronation Street with Ena Sharples! I thought I was hallucinating. My life was real rock and roll!

All the boys stayed on the bus, in the street outside the hotel, and when they woke up the bus was on bricks! The nice Glaswegian people had come and stolen all the wheels off the tour bus.

I thought I was better, but when we got to Doncaster and I was playing the sound check in the afternoon, I collapsed at the kit, completely unconscious. Glitter put me in his dressing room, they carried me in and he cleared out. The next thing I knew I woke up in Doncaster hospital on a drip. The doctors said I had ridiculously high levels of glucose in my blood and was all over the show! They did what they needed to get me back to normal. They wanted to know what on earth I had been taking. I explained what I'd been living on, Sanatogen and Lucozade. I had glucose poisoning! It's amazing how ill it can make you. I had no idea.

After that I had to start eating some food. Which is quite difficult when you haven't got a lot of money. But we thought we were taking the healthier option.

CROQUE-MADAME

Ingredients: serves 6

Brioche
15g fresh yeast
15g water
25g caster sugar
250g 00 flour
5g fine sea salt
3 eggs, lightly beaten
150g soft butter cut into cubes

Sandwich
6 slices of brioche
3 slices of Ogleshield cheese
1 small fresh truffle, optional
soft butter for spreading

Parmesan cream
1/2 leaf gelatine, soaked in cold
    water to bloom
100ml whipping cream
250ml milk
50g parmesan, grated

6 very thin rashers of dry cured
    streaky bacon or pancetta
6 large free range eggs
a small handful of chives, chopped

To make the brioche, dissolve the yeast in the water with the sugar. Put the flour and salt in the bowl of a mixer, and using the paddle attachment beat in the yeast mixture, followed by the eggs. Once a smooth batter consistency is achieved, start adding the butter one piece at a time until it's all incorporated.

Shape into a ball and place in a floured bowl. Cover with cling film and chill it in the fridge overnight. Remove from the fridge and shape into a greased and floured loaf tin. Leave in a warm place to prove for a couple of hours, or until the dough rises to just above the tin. Bake at 180°C for 30-40 minutes. Cool on a wire rack.

To make the sandwich, slice the brioche into 6, discarding the end crusts. Take 3 of the slices and lay your cheese on each. Cover with thinly sliced truffle if using and then top with the other slices of brioche. Spread the butter on the both of the outsides of the sandwiches. Brown each side of the sandwiches in a frying pan and then transfer to a 180°C oven for 5 minutes.

To make the parmesan cream, soak the gelatine in cold water to bloom. Heat the cream and milk in a small saucepan, remove from the heat, and then using a hand blender, blend in the parmesan and the gelatine. Pour into a cream whipper gun and charge with one gas canister.

Lay the bacon rashers between 2 baking trays and cook in a 180°C oven for 15-20 minutes until crisp.

Using an egg topper, remove the tops of the eggs, making sure you keep the rest of the shell intact. Discard the whites leaving the yolks in the shells. Cover the tops with cling film, stand them carefully in egg cups and steam them for 3 minutes.

To serve, cut the sandwiches into soldiers. Season each yolk with a few grains of sea salt. Fill each egg with the parmesan cream and stick a bacon crisp into each. Garnish with chives.

WE DID THIS DISH FOR A NEW YEAR'S EVE MENU. IT HAS ALL
THE ELEMENTS OF A CROQUE MADAME, EGG, CHEESE, BACON,
TOAST, SO WE CALLED IT THAT FOR FUN. YOU COULD DO IT
IN A LITTLE RAMEKIN RATHER THAN THE FIDDLY SHELL

BIG-IN-JAPAN

RECIPES

THE BLONDES WERE TRYING TO
BUILD, AND GET ON THE RADIO

"It was all going well, but like all things, there's a point when nothing is happening. I got frustrated. People like Pete and Buffin were asking me to do other things. The Damned were going on tour and Captain Sensible asked me to go as keyboard player. I can't fucking play keyboards! He said it didn't matter, which it wouldn't have done in The Damned, to be fair."

i was being asked to do things like that, odds and sods, some TV, video and session work

HEARTBREA

"I think the band felt like I was doing a lot of stuff they weren't. And I was getting frustrated as I wanted to do more."

It was only really me and Jeff, the singer, pushing at the time. So I left the band and they got another drummer. It never really worked out for them. But I felt I needed to move up to the next level.

A couple of guys I'd met had a band called Panache, who were absolute shit, but they had a Japanese record deal with Toshiba EMI. They had an album out but the drummer, this Japanese guy Paddy Phield who used to be the drummer in Cuddly Toys, couldn't play. I knew that they had to deliver a second album and a tour and they asked me if I'd be interested. I got on really well with the bass player, Terry, and as he was a mate I said I'd do it. I did it to go to Japan.

So we rehearsed and we did an album. Once the album was out, we got ready to tour. We didn't really like the singer much, so we decided to get rid of him and I rang Jeff from the Blondes. I asked him if he fancied coming to Japan. The downside was he had two weeks to learn all the songs. We spent two weeks every day in rehearsal studios, with him learning the songs, and then off we went.

We got to Japan, and at the sound check at a massive arena in Tokyo, after we'd done all the checks and levels, they said, "Okay, now can we do another couple of numbers, we've got to get the levels for the mobile." I didn't know what they were talking about, but it was for a live album! We didn't even know they were going to record the shows for a live album. So there we were, in Japan, for about two weeks. We did 10 live TV shows, 10 or 12 radio shows, and umpteen photo sessions in between. We played a couple of nights in Tokyo, in Nagoya, Osaka. I was knackered, but it was such fun.

I'd tried Japanese food before because we had always had Japanese girls and Japanese journalists around, and they'd take us to places. I had discovered yakitori at a yakitori bar in Blandford Street, but it was the only Japanese food that I knew. They'd do yakitori chicken skewers, which was sweet like teriyaki. In the basement there was a tiny sushi restaurant. We did go there one night and the chef sent us out a big marble platter, it looked like a Japanese garden, it looked beautiful. But everything on it was raw! And I just couldn't do it. I loved steak teriyaki, sweet glazed stuff, yakitori, shabu-shabu, tempura, vegetables and prawns. That was Japanese food to me, but when I discovered raw fish I thought I'd stay away from it. And seaweed. Who eats seaweed?

So when I got to Japan I needed a bit of guidance. Snoopy, a good friend and DJ who was part of the tour, told me about tonkatsu, breadcrumbed pork. And we used to live on noodles. I did eat great food, but none of that raw stuff, and none of that smelly seaweed. I remember walking down the street and finding vending machines, which I'd never seen. Vending machines where you could buy whisky or beer or anything really. 24 hours a day out of a vending machine that hadn't been vandalised. Amazing! In Japan I got introduced to lots of whisky, tons of sake, which I loved, hot or cold, and Japanese sweet plum wine, which is just heavenly stuff.

"I was 20. It was in '82. The Falklands war was on, and I remember being in TV studios where we were playing and there were news monitors."

But we were in Japan, doing live TV shows, the equivalent of Tiswas, getting chased with custard pies by mad Japanese people. We did a record signing in a store that was the equivalent of the HMV shop in Oxford Street. And it got so out of control around the building, in the streets, that they couldn't get us out of the building for the thousands of screaming kids outside. So we had to go up on the roof, to get a helicopter off the roof to get us out of the building, and I could hear the screaming from up there. It was just bizarre.

Trying to get away from a crowd, when you're running and they're screaming, you'd think it's funny, but it's actually really scary when you're getting grabbed at and you could get ripped to pieces. But then we'd get in the bus and they just banged on the window. Then it's great, waving out the window to loads of kids taking pictures. And us sat there drinking bottles of sake.

We'd get to the hotel and have to be snuck in the back and through the kitchens because in the lobby and outside the hotel are masses of kids. We had to have a whole floor of the hotel because kids would book on our floor, and the floor below and above, and we were under strict instructions not to touch. So you have to be careful, but who's careful at 20 years old living some surreal existence?

You do feel kind of untouchable.

It was a mad time and we were taken to a couple of really good clubs that every band used to go to. Everything was free. I didn't have to pay for anything anywhere I went. I just thought it was anybody English but it was obviously because we were in the band. So we'd go into a nightclub and all our drinks were free, all our food was free, and they'd lay out big banquets because we were coming. Japanese hospitality.

At home McDonald's used to shut at ten, half ten. And suddenly I was in a nightclub that didn't stop 'til 7 o'clock in the morning. I'd never heard of a place that was open 'til 7am. I suppose it was the VIP area. We were all just sitting, chatting. I remember being there with the Talking Heads and having a long conversation with their bass player, though I didn't know who she was. We were talking about tours and music. Weller was there, from The Jam. They weren't my heroes. But that's who I was in a club with, because they were on tour out there, and we were on tour. Thing is, they were cool. We were playing a load of shit, we weren't cool. We were a little teeny bop band. But we were massive, just in Japan, and I didn't care how embarrassing it was because no one was ever going to see it at home, no one was ever going to know about it.

Unfortunately thanks to the internet, people do know now, people can find it.

While we were in Japan, a guy called Lea Hart was out there touring with a Japanese artist, Ann Lewis. Ann Lewis was a huge Japanese star, on TV all the time and Lea Hart and the Rollups were the backing band. Me and Terry chatted with Lea in the studio because we were mates. And obviously the band we were with was shit, we knew that, he knew that. So we talked about doing something decent, a proper rock band. We decided that when he'd finished what he was doing in Japan and we'd finished the Panache tour, we would hook up and we'd form a proper band. We didn't know he was a bit of a con man. He'd had contracts to fulfil, he was the Arthur Daley of rock, he was a wheeler-dealer. He'd sorted out a little tour in Bangkok and then another one in India. But they were for Lea Hart or Lea Hart and the Rollups band. So we went as his band. We formed Ya Ya afterwards, but first we had to be the Rollups.

MISO-GLAZED-MACKEREL, SPICED-CUCUMBER, YUZU-MAYONNAISE

Ingredients: serves 8

Miso glaze
300ml dry white wine
180ml mirin
200g white miso paste
150g golden caster sugar
25g fresh ginger, grated
2 cloves of garlic, peeled
    and grated
60ml soy sauce

Spiced cucumber
10g fine sea salt
1 large cucumber, diced
10g soy sauce
10g fish sauce
2 cloves fresh garlic, peeled
    and grated
5g fresh ginger, grated
1 small carrot, cut into
    fine julienne
1 spring onion, finely sliced
5g Aleppo or Espelette
    pepper flakes
20g crushed peanuts

Yuzu mayonnaise
1 large free range egg and 1 yolk
1 tbsp white miso paste
20g yuzu juice
250g rapeseed oil
salt and white pepper

8 mackerel fillets, pin bones
    removed
a small handful of coriander

To make the miso glaze, put everything into a saucepan and reduce to a coating consistency. Leave to cool.

To make the spiced cucumber, sprinkle the salt over the diced cucumber and leave to drain for an hour.

Mix the soy, fish sauce, garlic and ginger. Add the carrot, onion, cucumber and pepper flakes.

To make the mayonnaise, put the egg and yolk, and miso paste into a blender or food processor. With the motor running, slowly trickle in the oil. Add the yuzu juice and season.

To serve, generously brush the miso glaze over the skin of the mackerel fillets and place under a very hot grill until the skin looks blistered and the fish is cooked through. Remove from grill and brush on some more glaze.

Spread some mayonnaise onto your plates. Put a spoon of spiced cucumber on each. Sprinkle the peanuts over the cucumber then place a warm mackerel fillet on each. Garnish with coriander.

THIS MISO GLAZE CAN BE USED ON A MYRIAD OF DISHES, AND YOU CAN USE BEER, CIDER, WHATEVER SUITS WHAT YOU ARE GOING TO DO WITH IT. THE RECIPE WAS GIVEN TO ME BY MY OLD MATE LUKE DALE ROBERTS, WHO NOW HAS THE TEST KITCHEN IN SOUTH AFRICA

THE iDEA BEHiND THIS WAS TO CREATE SOMETHING liGHT AND
JAPANESE iNFLUENCED, WiTH DASHi. i WANTED THE BROTH TO
BE POURED AT THE TABLE, TO REFERENCE THE JAPANESE
TEA CEREMONY. YOU CAN iNCLUDE ANY FiSH, SQUiD OR SHELLFiSH

Ingredients: serves 4

20-30 cockles

Dashi broth
500ml water
1/2 sheet of dried kombu seaweed
5g katsuoboshi (dried bonito flakes)
2 tsp soy sauce
1 1/2 tsp mirin
3g fine sea salt

Pickled seaweed
100g mixed seaweed
150ml rice wine vinegar
50ml water
50g golden caster sugar
5g fresh ginger, grated

Sea sponge
50g onion, peeled, diced
    and sweated in olive oil
2 large free range eggs
30g isomalt
10g plain flour
1g baking powder
25g cuttlefish ink

Algae
30g tapioca
10g dried nori powder

4 fillets of halibut, roughly
    160g each

Clean the cockles thoroughly under cold water to remove any sand and grit.

To make the dashi broth, bring the water and kombu to just below boiling. Remove from the heat and add the bonito flakes. Leave to steep for a few minutes, then pass through a fine sieve. Season with the soy, mirin and salt.

To make the pickled seaweed, wash the seaweed thoroughly. In a non-reactive pan, bring everything else to the boil, cool slightly then pour over the seaweed.

To make the sea sponge, put everything in a blender and blitz until completely smooth. Pour into a cream whipper gun and charge with one gas canister. Store in the fridge until required.

Fill a small plastic pudding mould or paper cup about half full with the sponge mix. Microwave for about 1 minute at full power or until the sponge rises to the top of the mould for a few seconds. Repeat the process one sponge at a time. Once cooled a little, remove from the moulds and tear into pieces.

To make the algae, put the tapioca in a pan of water to cover and boil until swollen and translucent. Wash under running water to remove all the starch then stir in the nori powder.

Season the fish fillets then gently steam them in a little of the dashi broth for a few minutes, or until just cooked. Steam the cockles in a very hot covered pan, until they just open.

To serve, place the fillets in the centre of your warmed bowls, spoon some tapioca around, arrange a few cockles in the bowls, along with the pieces of sponge, then drape with the seaweed. Pour in the remaining hot dashi broth.

GO-EAST

THE FOOD in BANGKOK is AMAZING

"We were taken to the sort of places you shouldn't go. I remember going off with some bloke on a motorbike."

We were in search of Thai stick, which is seriously hallucinogenic. We'd never had it but we'd heard about it. We could have been taken anywhere, by gangsters up the side street on a motorbike. I remember this room with a creaky old ceiling fan, and my brother passed out, just laying on a bed. He looked really pale and we were shaking him, we actually believed he was dead. I was panicking about what I was going to tell my Mum, when he suddenly sat up and went, "I can hear you, you know." That's the only thing like that I've ever done. Never again, but it was kind of funny.

Another time we were taken to an underground drinking club. It was in the depths of a shitty old hotel, like an old boiler room, and there were loads of tables and people sat around drinking and smoking. It was really seedy, but quite cool too. A Swiss or Austrian bloke sat with us and introduced himself. He was the nicest bloke. It turned out he was the head chef at the world famous Oriental hotel, where they do Thai cookery courses. While we were drinking there were police turning up on their motorbikes and everyone knew everyone. It's a bit of an eye-opener when you're young, the corruption, how gangland and prostitution and police were all one. But it didn't feel threatening in there.

It got late, and the chef offered to take us back to get some food. This chef from the most famous hotel in the world, takes us back to his house, to meet his wife, who cooks us all this food. It was fucking amazing! It was little sautéed things, bits and pieces, but it was really good. It tasted like nothing I'd ever had. We talked about going to the hotel and doing the Thai cookery course. Of course I never had time, but it was an open invitation.

I remember a fierce heat on everything I ate. I loved chilli and noodles, so was at it straight away. I got this big clay pot of noodles and broth and there were all these condiments to put on. I remember eating that and just burning my head off. I mean I'd never experienced anything so hot in all my life. I couldn't finish it. But it's all got that flavour. In Bangkok there is food literally everywhere in the street. You cannot move without a food market, or someone cooking, things on sticks, they're glazing, and putting things on the grill. And that smell, the smell of sweet meat and fish.

We used to get a bus from Bangkok down to Pattaya Beach. It's only a couple of hours and we'd have a few beers on the bus. We'd walk into the first hotel, check in, get changed, run straight out, hire jet-skis. There was one little beach that was a bit more secluded, where you could get a pitch and they'd come over and set you up a little camp. They would cook for you, chicken, beef or whatever, and you'd get a bowl of noodles with peanuts in, like a pad Thai. Then they'd come along and give you a pedicure, and then just as the sun was setting a lady would come out and she'd put a little grill down, she'd light a charcoal fire, put a rack over it and she'd cook things like fresh cuttlefish. We'd sit there and eat fresh fish on the beach and drink more beers. When we paid our bill it cost us something in the region of £1 each for the whole day, for everything, beers, the lot.

When I came back, I used to make noodles, like Malaysian nasi goreng. I'd put a fried egg on the top, whack a lot of fresh coriander in it and it just reminded me of that time. I've got a Thai dip that I learnt from that chef. It's just a little bit of soy, sugar, coriander, chilli, a simple Thai dipping sauce. When I first started cheffing, I remember making that, and using it as a dressing for everything in the restaurant.

Things are so different in the UK now to what it was like then; street food was a Westler's hot dog van, or flabby burgers outside the Odeon. There was no such thing as street food. Street food was something you ate at a football match and you knew you would get ill from a hot dog. Even restaurant food was pretty poor.

So we went to Thailand with Lea and then had to tour India with him. In between, we were due to go to Sri Lanka but the promoter died, so we decided to take couple of weeks' holiday in Bangkok and just partied. When it came time to go home we were on cheap flights, as we'd arranged that ourselves and we'd chosen Bangladeshi airline Biman.

They were a joke. We were aiming for the UK, but took off and flew to somewhere in India, and then ended up in Pakistan. We got to wherever the hell we were and they told us we were just stopping to refuel, that we should all get off for an hour. We were ferried into a room, then they locked the doors. It was sweltering hot, and we couldn't get out. The plane then obviously flew another load of people that had been sat there for a few days. They didn't have enough planes. We didn't know at that point what was going on, but we were pushed from pillar to post. It started off being a bit of a laugh, but then we were really thirsty and really hungry. They took us to a hotel, the scummiest place ever. We were given food that was moving and a jug of water with things swimming in it.

Finally we were taken back to the airport, but then we were left waiting again. We didn't go anywhere for days. I remember meeting people, some said they'd been there five days, others a week. We finally got on a plane and thought we were on our way home. But we stopped somewhere else. It took us weeks to get home. In the meantime, we had no possessions, nothing.

We were growing beards. We couldn't wash. We were chucked in and out of rooms. There were women with babies crying. Of course in the end tired, irritable and British, we were having none of it. They had all our passports and I can remember climbing over the immigration barrier and demanding our passports, grabbing passports and throwing them out to crowds of people.

In one room there was an old Coca Cola refrigerator with a padlock on it. I got an old metal table and managed to smash the lock open and start doling out these drinks to everyone. There were women and babies crying with thirst. Security came in, the doors had been locked on us, and me and Terry managed to break out. We started walking to the plane, to get our bags off, or at least our hand luggage. We walked out of the airport and across the runway back to the plane. And they start coming after us with those silly old rifles, elephant guns we sold them after the Second World War. They were yelling stop, stop or we'll shoot, and we just carried on. I was shitting myself, but Terry said just keep moving, don't look around, just keep doing what you're doing. Keep your hands by your side, keep them visible the whole time, don't make any sudden movements, we're fine. We got to the plane, walked up the steps and got on before we were arrested. They pinned us down in the aisle. At that point I asked Terry how he knew what we should do. He said he'd seen it in a Clint Eastwood film!

Our plan was to hijack the plane, and demand food, drink, and a bathroom. But we obviously couldn't fly it and they were the ones with guns in their hands. It was quite funny, until we were sprawled out with a gun in the backs of our heads. They put us in a little car and took us back to the airport, where we got a round of applause.

"In the meantime, Jackie and my Mum and Dad were all tearing their hair out at home, because we'd disappeared off the radar on a plane. There was no trace. They were phoning the airport, British Airways, they were phoning everyone. No one had any trace of it. Apparently Biman weren't allowed to land in certain places, they weren't a member of the Aviation Authority."

WE WERE AWOL

On one plane we hit a thunderstorm. I remember looking out the window and the sea was close, I was terrified. You could see the reflection in the water, of the lights on the wings flickering on and off. And there was lightning. They said an engine had gone. I reached for my life jacket, but Lea couldn't find his. We always used to carry one-sided razor blades. Not for drug abuse, in the studios you used to get them for splicing the tapes. When we went to Bangkok we used to tape razor blades to our pockets. Because there are loads of pickpockets out there, so if you got dipped, they'd cut their fingers, and not get your stuff. Anyhow, Lea hung on to me and cut my life jacket, because if he didn't have one I wasn't having one either. That's what he was like.

We managed to get through the storm and land again, by which time we'd made friends with a war correspondent, a journalist. I don't know how, but he managed to get word to the British Consulate, who sent an envoy out to meet us, who said that they would get us home. We were on our way home, but for some reason via Athens! So instead of home we were in yet another hotel room. It had shared rooms, with wire beds, and I remember pulling back the cover on the mattress and finding cockroaches. I went outside, sat on these steps and started to break down, uncontrollably sobbing. I physically couldn't take anymore.

And the next day the plane landed in fucking Amsterdam! Nothing to worry about, it's just a one-hour stop over, but you've got to get off. We tried to refuse, but in the end we did, it's a civilised airport. They changed the crew, and had some of the same crew come on who had pinned us to the floor in Pakistan.

Before they floored us we discovered that they had all the food and drink for the passengers stashed in their bags, the crew had nicked everything and said there was nothing. We'd had a bit of a fight with them about that, but we hadn't seen that crew since. After they saw us in Amsterdam airport, there was a bit of a fracas. Terry ran down the moving walkway behind one of the guys, and grabbed the hand rails, lifted a foot up and kicked him in the back between the shoulder blades. He went sprawling. Back on the plane, suddenly there was no take-off. On get the Dutch police. The guy from the air crew is with them and comes and points at us. We refused to move and said we'd not been off the plane. And everybody on the plane stood up and said we hadn't left the plane, which was amazing. The officials were infuriated, but they had to give up. The funny part is, as they turned around to walk away, the guy behind the policeman had Terry's trainer print right between his shoulder blades.

Anyway we finally landed about an hour later at Heathrow. Everyone had grown beards and looked totally dishevelled. We looked like we'd been on a desert island for a couple of weeks.

I got very ill, malaria, which I didn't know I had contracted through all this. I was staying at my Mum's, hallucinating, and in sweats. I was in a mess. I couldn't eat and drink. The doctor came round and wanted to know where I had been, what vaccinations I'd had? I hadn't had anything, but I'd been everywhere. He gave me loads of drugs and it took me a good few weeks to feel even slightly normal.

"At home going to an Indian was vindaloo or biriyani and that was it."

We had an Indian tour booked, we were going to play where The Police had recently toured. I didn't want to go. But the tour was booked and as the days went by I got slightly better, I knew I had to do it. So I got myself up, packed and sorted, and we flew to Bombay. It was Bombay then, not Mumbai. And funnily enough it was really good; it was a different experience.

When we got there I remember posters and a banner in the street welcoming us, and every gig was a big open-air theatre. The Police had done a thing called Police in the East. There's a documentary film of it, they were the first western band to go and play most of those places. It was open to us to do the same tour. It was an experience. We played Bombay, Bangalore, Punna, Goa and then back to finish in Bombay again.

One night there were English voices shouting at us from the audience. It was the British Navy. A big ship had had a collision on its way back from the Falklands and was in dock being repaired out there. All the sailors were at the gig. They were in dock for ages and were a bit stir-crazy. They invited us back to have a look at the battleship. We had a bit of a mad time in Bombay with the British Navy, I'm amazed I'm still alive really.

Everywhere we were taken to eat in India we had Chinese food! It was the same in Thailand. Whenever we were taken out in Thailand or India by the record company, it was always for Chinese food. I kept saying I wanted to eat authentic Indian food, and I was told that I couldn't eat what local people eat. I wanted to know why not. Our Indian promoter eventually asked me if I'd noticed how many cats there were around and how many chickens.

He was trying to infer that I'd be eating cat. In the end they took us to a sterilised touristy Indian place. They wouldn't take us to what was authentic. They took us to where rich people would eat. So we did go to a couple of restaurants, and it was largely vegetarian food, which surprised me because I hadn't realised how much of India is vegetarian.

I discovered kulfi, and was introduced to paneer and a couple of new meat dishes. When I came back, we used to go to Khan's in Notting Hill. We'd drive from East London to Khan's because it felt like the only semi-authentic Indian restaurant in London at the time.

Goa was our last port of call before we went back to Bombay and it was very different. I remember cashew nuts and palm feni, I smuggled some of that out. It's basically moonshine, illegally brewed alcohol. It's disgusting. But it gets you. And eating those fresh cashew nuts, like I'd never had before, so completely different to buying a packet of some stale shit over here. And the whole Portuguese influence in Goa, using vinegar. I learnt then about vindaloos, what they were. At home it was just about how hot something was, not the recipe. I didn't realise those words meant anything.

But the biggest food discovery for me in India was mangoes. Proper mangoes. Now we use Alphonso mangoes whenever they are in season, and that's all we use.

JOHN-DORY, CAULIFLOWER, ONION-BHAJI, CURRY-OIL

Ingredients: serves 4

4 fillets of John Dory,
  roughly 160g each

Curry oil
50g onion, peeled and chopped
50g dessert apple, chopped
150g rapeseed oil
25g mild curry powder

Bhajis
10g salt
100g onion, peeled and finely sliced
20g potato, grated
75g gram flour
7g ground cumin
5g ground coriander
3g turmeric
3g mixed spice

Cauliflower purée
1/2 head of cauliflower
100ml milk
30g butter
salt and white pepper

fresh coriander leaves

Prepare the John Dory fillets by dividing each into two. Store in the fridge until needed.

To make the curry oil, chop the onion and apple into small pieces. Put into a small saucepan with a pinch of salt and one tablespoon of the rapeseed oil and sweat for 5 minutes. Add the curry powder and carry on cooking for 1 minute. Cover with rest of oil. Heat to 80°C. Remove from heat and cover with cling film. Leave to stand at room temperature for at least 1 hour. This stage can be prepared 1 or 2 days in advance and the oil kept in the fridge before being passed through a sieve. The finished oil can be stored for weeks and used to flavour other recipes or to make curry mayonnaise.

To make the bhajis, sprinkle salt over the sliced onion and potato. Leave in a colander for a minimum of 30 minutes before squeezing out as much liquid as possible. Mix the gram flour and spices together, then add to onion and potato mix to form a sticky batter.

To make the cauliflower purée, divide the cauliflower into florets discarding the stalk. Slice the florets, put into a small saucepan, cover with milk and simmer until soft. This should take about 12 minutes. Place cauliflower and any remaining cooking liquid in a blender and purée. Add the butter and season with salt and white pepper. Carry on blending until silky smooth. Keep warm.

Form the bhaji mix into small golf-ball-sized balls and deep fry at 180°C for approximately 90 seconds until crisp and golden. Drain onto kitchen paper and keep warm.

Whilst the bhajis are frying start cooking the fish. Season the fillets then fry skin side down in a little vegetable oil until they look about two-thirds cooked. This will take around 2 minutes. Flip them over and cook for another 10 seconds then remove from pan.

To serve, place the fillets in the centre of your warmed plates, spoon some cauliflower purée on either side of the fish, place your bhajis next to each spoon of cauliflower then drizzle a little of the curry oil around each plate and garnish with coriander leaves.

THE FLAVOURS HERE JUST WORK. YOU COULD USE A DIFFERENT
FISH FOR THIS, BUT I LOVE JOHN DORY IF YOU CAN GET IT,
AND YOU CAN VARY THE BHAJIS BY USING DIFFERENT
VEGETABLES, CARROT AND FENNEL ARE GREAT TOGETHER

SPICED-ROAST-LAMB, SHEEP'S-CURD,MINT-SAUCE

THIS DISH RELATES TO DISHES IN GOA, WITH THEIR SPICING AND VINEGAR. YOU THINK THIS AMOUNT OF VINEGAR WILL DESTROY THE LAMB, BUT IT'S DELICIOUS. WE USE RUMP, BUT YOU COULD DO A WHOLE LEG ON THE BARBECUE. THE MINT IS A CLASSIC BRITISH ADDITION TO LAMB, BUT IT'S ALSO IN MANY CHUTNEYS

Ingredients: serves 6

6 trimmed, boneless lamb rumps
about 170g each

Marinade
30g sea salt
10g dried red chilies
1 tsp cumin seeds
3 pieces of cassia bark
4 cloves
30g fresh ginger
60g garlic cloves, peeled
and crushed
300ml white wine vinegar
3 bay leaves

Mint sauce
1 tbsp white wine vinegar
1 tsp sugar
1/2 tsp fine sea salt
freshly ground black pepper
1 bunch mint leaves,
finely chopped
1/2 bunch coriander leaves,
finely chopped
50ml extra virgin olive oil

Squash purée
1 butternut squash, peeled
5g fine sea salt
25g butter
freshly ground white pepper

150g sheep's curd or 1 small
fresh sheep's milk cheese
a small handful of coriander

To make the marinade, using a spice grinder or powerful blender, grind the salt, chili, cumin, cassia and cloves to a powder. Rub all over the lamb.

Grind the ginger and garlic to a paste then rub onto the lamb. Pour over the vinegar, throw in the bay leaves, and then leave in the fridge to marinate for a couple of hours or overnight.

Put the lamb and marinade in a covered non-reactive saucepan or casserole and cook in a very low oven, no more than 100°C for 90 minutes to 2 hours.

To make the mint sauce, mix the vinegar, sugar, salt and pepper together in a small bowl. Stir in the finely chopped herbs then gradually beat in the oil until it all comes together.

To make the squash purée, peel the squash, and slice the thinner end into six discs. Remove the seeds from the bulbous end, then slice it in small pieces.

Sweat the chopped squash in a little olive oil with 1/2 teaspoon of salt. Cover with a lid and continue to cook until completely soft.

Transfer to a blender and blitz until very smooth. Add the butter to make it rich and glossy along with a few grinds of pepper.

Fry the discs in a little oil and butter until nicely coloured on both sides and soft in the middle.

Remove the lamb from the pot and pat dry. Heat a little vegetable oil in a pan and fry the lamb; or, even better, using a hot grill pan or barbecue, sear the lamb all over, to give it a little charred appearance and barbecued flavour.

To serve, place a roast disc of squash in the middle of each plate. Carve the rumps, and place on top of the squash. Pipe or spoon the purée around the lamb along with the fresh curd. Serve the mint sauce separately. Garnish with coriander.

OLIVE-OIL-BRAISED CUTTLEFISH, PEAS, IBERICO-HAM

Ingredients: serves 4-6

400g cuttlefish, cleaned
3 cloves of garlic, peeled and
    finely sliced
100ml extra virgin olive oil
4 sprigs of thyme
1 bay leaf
fine sea salt
Espelette pepper
100ml dry white wine
150g peas
1/2 small bunch of flat leaf parsley
1 bunch of spring onions,
    finely sliced
a few fine slices of Iberico ham

To make the braised cuttlefish, slice the cuttlefish into strips, rings, squares or any shape that takes your fancy. Slice the garlic into fine slivers.

Using a pressure cooker, gently fry the garlic in the olive oil for 1 minute before adding the cuttlefish. Gently sauté the fish just until it starts to turn translucent, for about another minute. Add the thyme and bay leaf and then season with salt and Espelette. Pour over the wine and enough cold water to just cover.

Seal the lid and bring to full pressure. Cook for 10 minutes then leave until de-pressurised.

Boil the peas in salted water before draining and adding to the cooked cuttlefish. Finely chop the parsley leaves and add them to the pot.

To serve, ladle into warm bowls, sprinkle over the spring onions and top with slivers of the best Iberico ham you can find.

THIS IS VERY SPANISH IN ITS FLAVOURS. IT STARTED LIFE AS A
SAUCE, NOT A WHOLE DISH, BUT IT STOOD UP ON ITS OWN.
JUST WINE, WATER, GARLIC AND OIL WITH THE CUTTLEFISH
IN THE PRESSURE COOKER CREATES THIS SOFT AND YIELDING
THING. IT'S A BIT OF A REVELATION

PICKLED-PIGEON, NETTLE-QUINOA

THE SPICING ON THE MEAT IS GREAT WITH THE VINEGAR, IT DOESN'T OVERPOWER, BUT ADDS TO IT. ONCE THE REST OF THE GAME SEASON ENDS WE STILL HAVE PIGEON, AND THEY ARE REALLY GOOD IN SPRING. AND NETTLES ARE GOOD AT THE SAME TIME

Ingredients: serves 8

1 tsp coriander seeds
1 tsp cumin seeds
1/2 tsp black peppercorns
1/2 tsp chilli flakes
1/2 tsp salt
4 wood pigeons
a knob of butter
a little vegetable oil

Pickle

3 cloves garlic, peeled and sliced
1 bay leaf
1 tsp of sugar
300ml water
300ml Cabernet Sauvignon vinegar

Pigeon vinaigrette

the legs from the pigeons
300ml brown chicken stock
30ml pigeon pickling liquor
25ml hazelnut oil

Pickled vegetables

100ml Moscatel vinegar
50ml dry white wine
50ml water
50g golden caster sugar
1 bay leaf
1 sprig of thyme
5g fine sea salt
1 large carrot, peeled and cut
    into thin rounds
1 banana shallot, peeled and
    sliced into rings
6 small cauliflower florets,
    thinly sliced

Nettle purée

400g of nettle tops
50g cream
100g water
100g butter

Quinoa

1 shallot, peeled and chopped
100g quinoa
400g chicken stock
1 tsp fine sea salt

8 French breakfast radishes,
    thinly sliced

To prepare the pigeons, grind the coriander, cumin, peppercorns, chilli flakes and salt together and rub the mix all over the pigeon breasts. Cook the pigeons, breast side down, in a hot pan in a little oil and a knob of butter, until golden brown. Transfer the pan to 180°C oven and continue to roast for a further 8 minutes.

Leave to rest for 10 minutes before removing the breasts from the birds. They should still be quite rare.

Bring all the pickle ingredients to the boil and simmer for 3 minutes. Leave to cool until just warm then add the pigeon breasts. Leave to pickle for a couple of hours.

To make the vinaigrette, remove the legs from the pigeon carcasses. Cover with the chicken stock and reduce by two-thirds. Pass through a fine sieve. Return to the heat and whisk in 30ml of the pickling liquor from the breasts. Carry on reducing to a thin sauce consistency before removing from the heat and whisking in the nut oil. Keep warm.

To make the pickled vegetables, bring all the pickling ingredients to the boil before pouring over the vegetables.

To make the nettle purée, blanch the nettles in salted boiling water for 1 minute and refresh them in iced water. Squeeze all the excess water from them and put in the blender. Boil the cream, water and butter together and add it to the nettles and then blitz until very smooth.

To make the quinoa, sweat the shallot with the salt in a knob of butter until soft. Add the quinoa and cook for 1 minute. Add the stock and cook gently for 20 minutes, stirring occasionally until it's a porridge-like consistency. Add the purée.

To serve, spoon the quinoa onto each plate. Gently warm the pigeon breasts without further cooking them. Place one on each plate. Arrange a few of the pickled vegetables around, along with the radishes and a drizzle of vinaigrette.

ESCABECHE-OF-SEA-BASS

Ingredients: serves 4

Marinade
juice of 1 orange, and zest
    of 1/2 an orange
30ml Spanish Moscatel vinegar
60ml dry white wine
5g fennel seeds
5g coriander seeds
5g pink peppercorns
1 star anise
1 bay leaf
1 sprig of thyme
100ml extra virgin olive oil
sea salt flakes

1 bulb of fennel, sliced
1 banana shallot, peeled
    and sliced
1 large carrot, peeled and sliced
4 fillets of sea bass

To make the marinade, put all the ingredients (except the oil and salt) into a non-reactive pan and bring to the boil. Add the sliced vegetables and bring back to the boil then remove from the heat.

Season the fish on both sides then fry skin side down in a little vegetable oil. When the fish is about two-thirds cooked, turn the fillets over and continue to cook for 10 seconds before removing to a dish just big enough to hold the fish in one layer.

Whisk the olive oil into the marinade and add salt to taste.

Pour the warm dressing and vegetables over the fish and leave to cool.

This is great eaten at room temperature but will keep in the fridge for a few days and can be gently warmed under the grill.

To serve, place each fillet with the vegetables divided evenly between them. Whisk the remaining marinade to emulsify it a little, and then spoon over the fish and sprinkle with a few crunchy salt flakes.

THIS IS GOOD FOR HOME AS IT ISN'T LABOUR-INTENSIVE ON THE NIGHT. IT'S IMPORTANT NOT TO BOIL THE OIL, OR YOU WILL LOSE ITS FLAVOUR. YOU CAN VARY THE FISH, AND ALSO THE MARINADE, THE VINEGARS, THE OIL AND THE VEGETABLES

WE HAD A MANAGER CALLED IRA
BLACKER, A BIG AMERICAN GUY

LA-LA-LAND

Ira, our manager, used to run an agency in America in the 70s that was responsible for taking the first wave of British rock music to America. So the first bands they broke in America were people like Rod Stewart and the Faces. Then years later in the 80s he'd moved from the East Coast to the West Coast, and was living in LA and managing bands. I don't know how he came to hear of us but we went to meet him. He liked us, he became our manager and he kept putting us in touch with different songwriters and people to work with. So we started working with some of them, and off the back of what we'd done in India as Lea Hart and the Rollups, we then finally became Ya Ya. Ira started touting us around in America and signed us to a record company called Scotti Brothers. It was two brothers, proper American Italian boys. We used to call them Mafia Records, for obvious reasons.

Lea was going to LA, to mix and finish off the songs for our first record. And I went too because I was always with him in the studio. But the band didn't go, just me and Lea, and that was my first visit to America.

Ira put us in a motel. He lived in Marina Del Rey at the time, this big apartment block. I remember I'd heard of Marina Del Rey because Dennis Wilson, the drummer out of Beach Boys, had recently died, drowned in a boating incident on Marina Del Rey. So there we were in this apartment with all these windows looking out on the marina, up close to where Natalie Wood and Dennis Wilson died. It was odd but cool. It was an interesting place, lots of hanging out on the beach, and it's beautiful. That was my introduction to LA. I was a bit homesick to be honest, the first time I'd missed home. But in the studio it was cool. The studio we were mixing in was in Santa Monica. I remember the engineer's name was Tony, Tony Papa, and he had a Jeep, a Renegade.

I'd always wanted one. His was a silver Renegade open-top Jeep and he used to let me have a go and drive. I loved that. The studio was owned by the Scotti brothers. One day there I accidentally walked in on a meeting. A bunch of guys were standing around a table, jackets off due to the heat. All were in their shirtsleeves and wearing shoulder holsters with hand guns.

It was 1984, and MTV was still relatively new. In the lounge of the studio they had big TVs with stereo and MTV and I remember watching masses of videos of these bands I'd never seen before. I got a bit immersed in the culture, living near the beach, driving a Jeep and watching MTV.

It was a whistle-stop introduction to LA.

There were a few little incidents. We went out to a club in Hollywood one night and then drove back to Santa Monica, drunk. There was a police car and they made me stop, walk in a straight line, touch my nose, do all that stuff, it was scary. It was like India again! I've been arrested everywhere I've ever been, every city. In the middle of investigating us, the squad car got a call and they put their siren on and had to dash off. They told us to stand there, and then left us stranded. After a bit we thought, fuck them, and we left. Then they were suddenly swarming into our motel car park. Because we'd done a runner from a scene of a crime.

Times like that you become a bit like one of those people you read about, thinking you're invincible. Because even though it was 2 o'clock in the morning, or whatever time it was, we got our manager out of bed. He rang a guy called Herbie Herbert who was Journey's manager and Journey kind of owned San Francisco and the West Coast, they were that big. Herbie Herbert was well-connected with someone else and they got us this lawyer and we were fine.

LA was great for certain kinds of food. I remember Mexican restaurants, Tex Mex. Chilli was the thing at the time, it was the dirty food that was in. In LA there are Mexican places everywhere, with chilli dogs, chilli burgers, chilli everything. The first time I ordered chilli con carne, I didn't realise chilli con carne meant meat with chilli. Up came this big steak, like a T-bone, with a big, green chilli pepper. It wasn't that hot, but it was grilled and pinned to the top of the steak. I remember being hugely disappointed that it was not what I had ordered. But then I ate it and it was really good, I was chuffed.

I did learn a bit about the way Mexicans use chocolate, in mole sauces and the like. For me, using chocolate like that was weird. But I learned about chocolate being a major Mexican foodstuff, how they use it in everything. And when you taste a mole sauce, just finished with a bit of chocolate, you get it. From that day on I always put chocolate in my chilli.

In America shrimp is prawn and it could even be a langoustine, it's all shrimp to them. I remember ordering shrimps and getting a big plate of langoustines. I got quite into that because you couldn't do that at home. Ira took us to a fish market and bought buckets of scallops, then took us back to his apartment to cook them. They were incredible. That's the first time I remember eating scallops.

Opposite our motel were a few all-night cheap places, 7/11s and that sort of thing, which we didn't have here then. I remember there was Taco Bell. I remember trying it, because it was novel to us, it was crap but novel. Everything was covered in melted cheese and refried beans, and cream. And there was a doughnut place. We used to go across the road to get coffee there.

It's a cliché that police officers sit around eating doughnuts, but there were always coppers sat in there eating doughnuts.

I didn't like the doughnuts much because they were different. To me a doughnut came from Kossof's Bakers in Petticoat Lane, the best doughnuts you have ever had. You can still get the odd decent doughnut in the 24-hour bakery in Brick Lane. To me as a kid, a proper jam doughnut was the thing. And these things were soft, they didn't taste the same, they had no jam in them, they had glazes on and holes in the middle. Why is there a hole in it? They'd nicked the rest of my doughnut. To me a doughnut is a proper jam doughnut.

We used to give doughnuts with coffee in the restaurant, because everyone gives chocolates. I sometimes did filled ones, crab apple jelly doughnuts, all sorts. Doughnuts come from my childhood, and the cultural difference between American doughnuts and an English doughnut was interesting.

Surf and turf is another thing people think of as American. But I don't call meat and seafood together surf and turf, for me it comes from Spanish cooking. In Spain they put a lot of meat and fish together. I've not always done it because it became a little bit of a trend, the old monkfish and oxtail thing everyone does. I don't think that works. I don't like black pudding and scallops either, people say it works but I don't think so. Pork belly and scallops was always big for me, and I've done it in several guises. It does work, like scallops and bacon, which is a classic pairing. That is all it is, so it isn't weird. I've done pork belly with langoustines, and we do squid and chorizo, very Spanish. I will always put clams with pork but to me that is very Spanish again. So we do a fair bit, but only things that make sense to me.

WE HAD ALREADY DONE PHOTOS
FOR THE ALBUM BEFORE WE LEFT

"We had this idea for the cover, as we had called the album Scarred, to have a girl carving Ya Ya into her body. Self-harm wasn't such a big issue then. Actually we got Linzi Drew (who became editor of Penthouse), to do the photo. It's of her sitting there in all her gear, stockings and all that, at a dressing table, and the mirror is smashed, she's got a bit of mirror and she's cutting into herself."

"We got thousands of pictures and they're all her finest poses."

We also got pictures of Terry sat there in his underpants in the same poses, that was just us messing around.

So we thought the album cover was done and dusted. But when we got to America we got the bad news that the record company wasn't happy with it. Lea had also done a photo shoot before we left, of his arm with a full sleeve tattoo. It wasn't a real tattoo, it was good though. We reckon he knew about the cover already, and wasn't being open with us. And when the proofs for the album came, the cover was a picture of his tattooed arm. He must have known the other stuff had already been offed, and we didn't, we thought we had this amazing cover. The only time his plan came unstuck was when it came to Japanese release, some tattoos in Japan are a big no-no, they're associated with gangland mafia.

We finished mixing the album, and it was exciting to have a record finished and to have to decide what would be the single. Then the album got picked up by 20th Century Fox who were making the film Revenge of the Nerds. Ira managed to get us two songs in the movie. And then 20th Century Fox decided that our single would be the single released from the soundtrack album. We did a deal where they paid for us to do a video. It doesn't sound a lot now by video budgets, but it was £20,000. We shot it at the Brixton Academy, the same week George Michael shot Careless Whisper.

We wanted to tour America. And nothing ever happened. Lea had this reluctance; he'd lost his bottle. He had started drinking more and he didn't want to do anything, he had this kind of built-in self-destruct button. For everything really good that we were offered he'd want to take another route. It was a bit disappointing. The single was released in America, and started breaking into the Billboard charts.

For the English release, our record label was CBS, who had offices in Soho Square. It was weird, they welcomed us as if we were from America. They thought we were some shitty American rock band over to visit, and they had to do their bit for us. We had to break it to them we were English. The Scotti brothers were big news at the time because they'd just had a hit with Eye of the Tiger by Survivor, for the Rocky movie. So we were promoted here as an American band and that didn't really work for us.

The single did all right. Radio legend Tommy Vance, who used to do the Friday Rock Show for Radio One, latched onto us, as did some of the press, and he started playing the track. We did a session for Tommy and things really started to pick up.

We hoped we were going to tour America, and were in contact with Ira all the time. But in the meantime me and Ray the guitar player started trying to write. I remember the first song I wrote with him and it was sort of all right-ish. Then me and Terry wrote some lyrics together, and we put it together with Ray. We went round to Nick's studio, the old session keyboard player who'd worked on the first album, and we did a little demo. We'd written a couple of songs we liked, and along with Lea's song they went on a demo, which got played around by Ira. Bellaphon in Germany liked it and offered us a deal for £50,000 or something. Lea wanted to take it, as it was an independent deal. But we knew that a couple of other people had heard it, one being Warner Brothers. We met up with Warners and it turned out that the song they'd picked up on was one I'd written.

Rob Dickins was a major player in this country, the biggest man in the music biz at the time, the head of Warner Brothers in England. He had taken Van Halen, ZZ Top, Madonna and Prince, all from Warner Brothers America, and broke them huge in the UK, around '84/85. His next ambition was to take an English band and do the same thing with them in America.

What happened was that Rob Dickins was in the record company offices with Bill Drummond. Bill's an amazing eccentric guy, who managed loads of Liverpool bands, and later formed the KLF. They were having an argument about the promotional budget for one of Bill's bands. And there was this music playing in the background that he brought into the row. Bill turned around to Rob and said, "It's all right if it's a band like this, you spend all the money on them. But, you know, those guys don't need it, it's the little bands that do." He was assuming that the band they were listening to was a big American band. Apparently this heated argument kind of went quiet because then they looked at each other and went, "Who is that?" They went to the Head of A & R, Max Hole, to ask whose record he was playing. And it was us. So Rob Dickins decided to sign us to Warners and we were the band that he was going to break in America.

IBERICO-PORK-PRESA, RAZOR-CLAMS, WILD-GARLIC-BUTTER

PRESA IS ONE OF THE FINEST THINGS OUT THERE. IT'S RED WITH MARBLING, LIKE THE PORK VERSION OF WAGYU BEEF. IT'S A GREAT CUT, FROM JUST BEHIND THE SHOULDER AREA. IT ISN'T USED MUCH HERE, BUT IT'S EATEN IN SPAIN, AND THE FLAVOUR IS STUNNING

Ingredients: serves 4-6

Wild garlic butter
125g soft butter
20g parsley
1/2 banana shallot, peeled
    and chopped
50g wild garlic leaves
1/2 tsp fine sea salt
pinch of Espelette pepper

Razor clams
500g razor clams
glass of dry white wine

1 presa (approx 800g)
white or purple sprouting broccoli
fine sea salt and freshly ground
    white pepper to taste

To make the wild garlic butter, put all of the ingredients into a blender or food processor and blitz until smooth. Scrape into cling film and roll tightly to form a neat log. Store in the fridge until required.

Wash the clams under cold running water for a few minutes. Heat a wide shallow pan until it's really hot. Put in the razor clams and pour over the wine. Cover with a lid straight away to trap in the steam. Leave the clams to cook for 1 minute then drain through a colander. Keep the juices. Once the clams are cool enough to handle, remove them from their shells. Cut away the intestinal tract and foot of the clam, retaining only the nice white firm fleshy bits. Slice diagonally.

Heat a grill pan or barbecue. Coat the presa in a little olive oil and season with fine sea salt. Place on the pan or barbecue and cook for about 5 minutes on each side, turning occasionally, making sure it doesn't burn. Remove to a warm place and leave to rest for 10 minutes. It's at its best served medium rare or no more than pink. You could probe the thickest part if you have a meat thermometer. I find 59°C is about right. If the thought of eating pork cooked any other way than well done freaks you out, then I suggest cooking something else. Iberico pork is expensive.

To serve, quickly blanch a few pieces of sprouting broccoli for about a minute. Put them on the grill to finish cooking and give them a charred flavour, then season with fine sea salt and freshly ground white pepper.

Warm a little clam juice in a small pan, add a couple of slices of garlic butter and the sliced clams to gently warm.

Carve the pork into slices and place on warm plates with the broccoli. Spoon the clams and buttery juices over the pork.

ROAST-SCALLOPS, WILD-GARLIC-PESTO

Ingredients: serves 6

Wild garlic pesto
60g wild garlic leaves
20g flat leaf parsley
5g fine sea salt
30g roast, skinned hazelnuts
100ml olive oil

Cauliflower purée
1/2 head of cauliflower
100ml milk
30g butter
fine sea salt
freshly ground white pepper

12 scallops, removed from their
   shells and completely trimmed
a knob of butter
a little vegetable oil
a squeeze of lemon juice
fine sea salt
freshly ground white pepper
6 sprigs of white sprouting broccoli

To make the wild garlic pesto, put all the ingredients except the oil into a blender. Blitz for a few seconds whilst adding the oil, until it becomes a rough paste.

To make the cauliflower purée, divide the cauliflower into florets, discarding the stalk. Slice the florets, put into a small saucepan and cover with the milk, simmer until soft. This should take about 12 minutes. Place the cauliflower and any remaining cooking liquid in a blender and purée. Add the butter and season with salt and white pepper; carry on blending until silky smooth. Keep warm.

Roast the scallops on the hob using a little vegetable oil and a knob of butter. Don't overcrowd the pan as you want them crisp and golden. After a couple of minutes, they should be well browned on one side and about half cooked. Turn over, and roast for another minute. Baste with the buttery pan juices and a squeeze of lemon, and season. Drain on kitchen paper.

To serve, quickly blanch the broccoli in salted boiling water for a minute. Drain then toss in the scallop pan juices to dress. Put a swipe of purée on each warmed plate, with a few blobs of pesto, the scallops and a sprig of broccoli. If your wild garlic has flowers, you can use them to garnish the plate.

EVERYONE SAYS THAT HAND-DIVED SCALLOPS ARE THE THING.
BUT WHEN WE MOVED TO KENT I DISCOVERED RYE BAY SCALLOPS.
THEY HAVE THE MOST AMAZING FLAVOUR, REALLY SWEET.
THEY TASTE BETTER THAN A lot OF THE HAND-CAUGHT ONES

STEAMED-HARE-BUN, CHOCOLATE-SAUCE

WE WERE looking AT STEAMED CHINESE PORK BUNS AND DECIDED TO DO SOMETHING SIMILAR. INSTEAD OF GOING THE OBVIOUS ROUTE WE TRIED BRIOCHE DOUGH, WHICH CAME OUT LIGHT AND PERFECT. WITH THE RICH JUS IT MADE SENSE TO ME TO DO THE MEXICAN THING AND FINISH IT WITH A BIT OF DARK CHOCOLATE

Ingredients: serves 8

Bun filling

1 hare, loin fillets removed,
  separated into pieces, or
  4 hare legs
1 onion, peeled and roughly
  chopped
1 carrot, peeled and chopped
1 stick of celery, roughly chopped
250ml red wine
3 cloves garlic, peeled and chopped
1 large sprig of thyme
1 bay leaf
100ml port
1 litre game or brown chicken stock

Brioche

15g fresh yeast
15g water
25g caster sugar
250g 00 flour
5g fine sea salt
3 eggs, lightly beaten
150g soft butter, cut into cubes

2 squares of 100% dark chocolate
watercress
fresh horseradish

To make the filling, brown the hare in a little vegetable oil. Remove from pan then brown the vegetables. Deglaze the pan with the wine, add the garlic, herbs and port. Put the hare back in and cover with the stock. Season and cover with a circle of parchment paper and a tight-fitting lid. Braise in a low oven or on top of the stove for about an hour-and-a-half, or pressure cook for 30 minutes.

Leave to cool before passing through a fine sieve. Pick all the meat from the bones and flake into a bowl. Finely chop the cooked vegetables and add them to the meat. Reduce the stock to a sauce consistency. Reserve enough to just coat each bun and add any remaining into the flaked meat. Adjust the seasoning.

Using cling film, make 8 round faggots of the hare mixture weighing roughly 50g each, wrapping them tightly into round balls. Chill them in the fridge to set.

To make the brioche, dissolve the yeast in the water with sugar. Put the flour and salt in the bowl of a mixer and using the paddle attachment beat in the yeast mixture, followed by the eggs. Once a smooth batter consistency is achieved, start adding the butter one piece at a time until it's incorporated. Shape into a ball and place in a floured bowl. Cover with cling film and chill it in the fridge overnight.

Working with the dough straight from the fridge take large golf-ball-sized pieces and flatten them with your hands. Unwrap the hare balls and mould the brioche dough around them. This is best done one at a time to prevent the butter in the dough from melting and becoming sticky. Place on a bun or muffin tray and leave to prove for 15 minutes. Steam the buns for 20 minutes. Once steamed, they can be stored in the fridge and reheated if you don't want to eat them the same day.

To serve, place a warm bun in each bowl, warm the remaining sauce then, off the heat, whisk in one or two squares of chocolate until glossy and just detectable when you taste it. Check the seasoning then spoon over each bun to just coat. Top each bun with a sprig of watercress and a grating of horseradish.

DULCE-DE-LECHE
DOUGHNUTS

Ingredients: makes 6 large
or 12 mini doughnuts

350g dulce de leche
85ml milk
10g fresh yeast
45g golden caster sugar
300g plain flour
pinch of salt
1 large free range eggs,
    lightly beaten
30g butter, melted

To make the doughnuts, fill a squeezy bottle
with dulce de leche, you'll have some left over.

Warm the milk a little, dissolve the yeast in the
milk with a teaspoon of the sugar.

Put the flour, remaining sugar and salt into
the bowl of your mixer. Add the yeast mixture,
followed by the egg and the melted butter.

Carry on mixing at a medium speed for about 10
minutes or until the dough is smooth and coming
away from the sides of the bowl. Form the dough
into a ball and place in a greased bowl. Cover the
bowl with cling film and refrigerate it overnight.

On a floured board, roll out the dough to just
under a 1cm thick. Cover with cling film and put
it back in the fridge to chill and firm up a bit.

Using a pastry cutter of whichever size you fancy
your doughnuts, carefully cut and place them on
greased sheet. Leave them in a warmish place to
prove for about 30 minutes.

Set your fryer to 190°C. Carefully fry them in
batches, a few at a time, for a minute or two on
each side. Drain on some kitchen paper before
tossing in plain sugar, or sugar flavoured with
a little cinnamon.

To serve, once cool enough to handle, pipe the
dulce into the sides of the doughnuts. These are
best eaten straight away.

YOU CAN MAKE YOUR OWN DULCE DE LECHE IF YOU BOIL
UP A TIN OF CONDENSED MILK. BUT YOU CAN BUY REALLY
GOOD ONES, AND IT'S SAFER! YOU CAN STUFF THE DOUGHNUTS
WITH OTHER THINGS TOO, JAM, LEMON CURD, APPLE PUREE.
FILL THEM, DUST THEM, OR EAT THEM PLAIN

SUNSET - STROP

AS A RESULT OF BEING ROB
DicKiNS' BiG SiGNiNG, OUR AGENT
WAS SUDDENly HARVEY GOLDSmiTH

"Everything was big and the biggest, which was fantastic for us. Although a bit of a poisoned chalice, because then there was pressure. We did more demos, we went through producer after producer. Every time we'd get something done they'd tell us to try some other guy. We were writing and recording the album, mainly in and around London."

"Rob Dickins was out in
LA with Mike Chapman.
Rob rescued Rod Stewart's
career at around that time."

I say rescued, Rod had disappeared a bit. Rob had signed him, and was out in LA with him, working on songs. While he was out there Rob played Mike Chapman our stuff. Mike, apart from being half the Chinnichap songwriting team who wrote loads of successful pop stuff back in the 70s, was by this time a big producer, he had done all of the Blondie stuff. He produced a big American hit for the Knack, My Sharona, and he'd done all the Pat Benatar stuff. He was massive and Rob played him our stuff. He said he'd love to work with us.

So suddenly the five of us were shipped off to record in Cherokee studios, to work with Mike Chapman. They stuck us in the Sunset Marquis to live. Which was the rock and roll excess hotel. It was Oscars time I remember, because the parties were on. They used to have an Oscars party at Spago, which was Wolfgang Puck's place. Even then I had heard of Wolfgang Puck. I don't know how I had heard of him or why. I must have read about him in a magazine. I knew he was this celebrity chef in America. Spago used to be above a building in a car park that overlooked Tower Records on Sunset Boulevard. And I made a pilgrimage to Tower Records, because that was what you used to do, if you went to America you bought loads of records. I remember seeing the restaurant, but couldn't get in because it was a party or something.

Our hotel was crammed with movie stars and pop stars, but that was the norm in that hotel. I remember Phil Collins wandering in. I used to be a massive Phil Collins fan when I was young, as a drummer, not so much as a solo artist. One night, when we were pissed, we found out what room he was in, and kept ringing it. All night we woke him up and said, "Yeah, hello, is Bill there please?" We thought it was hilarious.

Obviously we got complaints eventually. But I remember years later watching a video of his on TV, it was for I Wish it Would Rain Down. He was playing a stage hand sweeping the stage and then standing there dreaming that he is a performer, seeing Variety magazine, and the headline is Bill Collins.

Mike was brilliant; when we went to the studio to do our take, we'd go in and start warming up, have a couple of run-throughs, blasting away, until we were ready. Then we'd say we were ready, and Mike would tell us to piss off, and go lie around the pool, go have lunch. He would record while we were doing our thing, while we were warming up, and then get us to bugger off. Then he'd spend all day sorting through it, chunking it together, to get a performance. He claimed that as soon as you think you are ready, you don't perform. We used to call him the vibe man, because he is really into the whole feel of things. Which we liked, we hadn't worked with anyone like that before.

He'd listen to the playback at the most excessive volume. I like things loud, but fucking hell, how could he even hear what was going on? But he wasn't listening for sounds; that came later, he was listening to what it felt like, if it rocked out. He was getting a groove going. I remember once, he threw me the keys to his beautiful yellow Rolls Royce Corniche, with whitewall tyres. It needed moving for some reason. I went down to the car park and put the key in the ignition and bang! He had one of the playback demos in his car to listen to on the way in. It nearly took my head off it was so loud!

So we got to spend lots of time around the pool. I walked out to the pool one day and the band were lying around. I was a bit bleary eyed and asked someone if they had any towels, and they just pointed.

I walked over to what I thought was the pool man, he was bending down and talking to someone swimming. He had a t-shirt on and jeans and boots. He looked like he was doing something with the hose, cleaning the pool. So I bent down and asked, "Where do I get the towels, mate?" He answered that he thought you had to go and ask over there. All these girls, came over to me and begged me to introduce them, they were desperate. It was fucking Bruce Springsteen! And I thought he was the pool attendant! He was very gracious. The guy he was talking to in the pool was a famous actor, Peter Boyle. He was in a film with Al Pacino, and I love Al Pacino, so I recognised him. He was in the pool. Bruce knows him. He's chatting to him, and there's me asking if I can have some more towels.

That was suddenly my life.

Spago was the hottest ticket in town, but on the other side of Sunset Strip there was a restaurant called Le Dome, which was also a cool place. We were booked in there for lunch, to meet Mike, just before we started recording. He had lunch there with Rod Stewart, with everyone. And I think he had another business meeting that morning. He was at the celeb table in the window. Our lunch was at 1 o'clock. Living at the Sunset Marquis, you have limo service. So we booked a limo. When we said that we had a lunch meeting at Le Dome, they looked at us a bit funny, and checked we wanted the limo. We said yeah and it turned up, a big white stretch limo and we all piled in. It was great, there were drinks in the back and phones, electric seats and windows, and we mucked about like a bunch of idiots. The driver drove to the end of the road, wound the shield down and asked if we'd like him to drive round town, or round the block a couple of times. We said that no, we had a lunch date to make. So he turned left and pulled over; we had hired a limo to cross the road!

We felt like a right bunch of bell ends, piling out in front of this big glass window. Mike Chapman was sitting there, and must have been thinking what a load of English pricks. He knew where we were staying. It was probably why he booked the restaurant.

We were rehearsing at a place called SIR in Hollywood, which was great. There was everything you needed, food and drinks. I walked off to go and get a coffee, and saw a room with a buffet, coffee and sandwiches, and people sitting around eating and drinking. So I wandered up, and started helping myself. This really nice lady came up to me and said, "Oh yeah, fine, go ahead." Which I thought was strange, as I was already standing there stuffing myself. I looked up and recognised a guitar player called Waddy Wachtel, he is quite recognisable, with really long hair and round glasses. He is a big session man, and had played with Stevie Nicks for years. Then the penny dropped that I was actually standing in Stevie Nicks' rehearsal room, eating their sandwiches and drinking their coffee. I had seen them all standing there and assumed that was just where the food and drink was. If I had walked past their room, to the reception desk and to the right, there was coffee stuff, a machine, help yourself, not quite the buffet they had. It was quite embarrassing. I just stood there like a spare part and slowly backed my way out of the room.

Unfortunately, Mike's way of recording was great for us, but not for Lea. We'd been having problems with him through all of the London sessions. He was drinking more and more. We all were. But you still turn up for work. He was showing the signs, and it was affecting his work. He would never get up in the morning. I know that is a really rock and roll thing to do, and back in the day there were times when I got up and it would be dark,

but if you have got something to do you get up and do it. He would never get up. And his place was always in darkness, the curtains shut. He was becoming a pain in the arse, very hard to deal with.

Mike asked us to go off one day, he just wanted to see Lea for vocals. It was Lea's time to work. He wanted him in the morning, it sounded ridiculously early, but it was probably 10 or 11. He said he couldn't sing in the morning. Mike's reasoning was that when you wake up in the morning you have more of a vocal range. You haven't been drinking lots of tea or coffee, you haven't been speaking, your voice is fresher. He'd have got him going, a bit croaky maybe. But when Lea thought he was ready to start he'd have probably said, see you later. And he'd have had him at his purest. He protested, but Mike wasn't having any of it. We told him he had to do it, not go out the night before, get up in the morning, and do the vocals. It was singing three songs! We didn't trust him. We phoned his room in the evening, no answer. We put our ear to his door, and could hear the telly on, blasting out. We banged on the door, no answer. I am a bit of a sceptic, so I broke into his room. He had even put cushions under the covers in his bed, and his hat on the pillow. We went straight down to the Rainbow Room on Sunset, to the bar at the end. There was Lea, slumped over the bar, with a bottle of Jack Daniels, draped in strippers. Fine. But do your singing, then go do that.

We had a band meeting, we had had enough leading up to this. And we just thought, enough is enough. So we decided to sack him, like you do, in the middle of an album, when you have been signed by Rob Dickins.

ASPARAGUS-CARBONARA

Ingredients: serves 4

Confit egg yolks
vegetable oil
4 duck egg yolks

Parmesan custard
50g freshly grated parmesan
2 large free range eggs
50ml whipping cream

20 spears of asparagus
6 thinly sliced rashers of dry-cured
    streaky bacon or pancetta
extra virgin olive oil
fine sea salt
freshly ground white pepper
20g piece of fresh parmesan

To confit the egg yolks, half fill a small saucepan with vegetable oil. Carefully add the egg yolks, making sure you keep them separate, and cook in the oven at 65°C for 1 hour.

To make the parmesan custard, put all the ingredients into a small saucepan. Cook over a low heat until thickened. This should take about 7 minutes.

Snap the woody ends off the asparagus spears, and then using a mandoline or vegetable peeler, slice each spear lengthways into thin ribbons.

Lay the bacon in a cold frying pan. Gently fry until it starts to release its fat before turning. Keep cooking and turning until crisp. Drain on kitchen paper.

To serve, cook the asparagus in plenty of salted boiling water for 30 seconds. Drain and quickly toss it in the olive oil, salt and pepper. Put a spoon of custard in the bottom of your warmed bowls. Place a mound of asparagus in the middle of each. Top with an egg yolk, snap the bacon rashers into halves and place around. Finish each dish by grating parmesan over the top.

MY FIRST DISCOVERY OF BRUNCH WAS AT HUGO'S, AN ITALIAN PLACE AROUND THE CORNER FROM THE SUNSET MARQUIS. THEY HAD THIS DISH OF TAGLIATELLE WITH EGGS, BACON AND SPINACH, LIKE A CARBONARA. AT FIRST IT SEEMED WEIRD FOR BREAKFAST, BUT EGGS AND BACON WORK, AND THE NATURAL PARTNERS FOR ASPARAGUS ARE EGG AND CHEESE, PARTICULARLY PARMESAN

NEW-YORK, NEW-YORK

IT CAUSED A SHIT-STORM

"We told Mike that we'd had enough, and that we'd sacked Lea, he was really supportive."

I remember we were once in the middle of a song, and we needed some more words. Mike is a big hit songwriter, he had a number one song in America at the time this happened. He just said that he could put it together, but that we had written it all, those were our songs, they were great and we were more than capable of finishing it off. Whereas other producers, they'll change a word, just to get a writing credit. He didn't impose anything, but he could bring out the best in anyone. So Mike said, you gotta do what you gotta do, call me when you're done.

We had a management meeting with Ira and Lea. Lea had a very different view of things. When we spoke to Ira we realised that Lea had been feeding him bullshit and lying to him, as well as to everybody else. And when Ira found out some of the truths he was a bit shocked. Of course when the news filtered back to the UK, Rob Dickins hit the fucking roof. The guy in charge of us was now Bill Drummond. He flew straight out to try and sort the situation. He understood our point of view and sided with us, if there is taking sides in that sort of thing. It's like divorce, isn't it?

We came home and left Lea there. We left him in LA. We had to go and see the record company straight away. In the meantime we made a plan, we needed a new singer and we needed to carry on. A couple of years previously I'd seen a Geordie band called Emmerson. I remembered the singer Sam as he had a great voice. At that time we had said to each other how cool it would be if he was in our band. So we contacted him and he was interested. By this time he was in another band with a couple of people we knew. They had a gig in Kent, so Bill Drummond hired a car, and drove us all out to Gravesend, and we all walked in. Sam knew we were coming, and it was so obvious.

They came out onto this stage, and there was hardly anyone there in the audience, a shitty empty gig in Gravesend, except all of us, and Bill Drummond. The rest of the band were furious. Sam had a choice. We weren't big, but we had a big deal, and we had the potential to be big. He came on board and he sounded great. He did vocals on the tracks we'd done.

We went into Warner Bros and Rob Dickins wasn't having it. He felt we should give Lea a chance. We explained the way he had been behaving. He thought maybe it would be different when we heard ourselves on the radio, when he had a hit record, maybe then he would behave differently. We just didn't think we would ever get to that stage with him. We told him about our new bloke. But Rob Dickins felt there was no way you could have a rock band with a singer called Sam. Who has ever heard of a rock band with a singer called Sam! Funnily enough Sam's real name is Simon, but he's always been Sam. At the time Van Halen had famously fallen out with David Lee Roth. They came back with Sammy Hagar and became bigger than they ever were, on Warner Brothers. As Rob Dickins was standing there talking to us there was a huge Van Halen poster on the wall behind him. With Sammy Hagar. It was a bit of an epiphany. Sam was all right.

We had made our point, and worked on finishing the album, with Sam, and a producer from New York called Stephan Galfas. We got on great. He was also working with another band that included Tori Amos, and he wanted me to play with them. He needed a couple of vocals doing in America. So Sam had to go to America, to New York. I'd never been to New York, so of course he needed someone to go with him. So me and Sam took off to New York, to Skyline Studios, which was Nile Rodgers' studio.

SO THERE i WAS iN NiLE RODGERS'
STUDIO iN NEW YORK, WiTH SAM,
DOiNG A VOCAL

Unfortunately the city that never sleeps pretty much shuts down in between Christmas and New Year, everyone buggers off. Come New Year's Eve we were scraping around trying to find something to do. There was an MTV New Year's party, Duran Duran were on, and Sam was trying to contact Andy Taylor so we could go to that. Sam used to be in a band with Andy Taylor back in Newcastle. Nothing was happening. We were walking around and could see them setting up the New Year's thing in Times Square. We thought that was too touristy. If I'd been in London I wouldn't have gone to Trafalgar Square. So we ended up in a bar up the road, but then it got to nearly midnight and we thought sod it, let's go and see what's going on. A riot kicked off, there were some gunshots, a woman screaming, and everyone running. The crowd had dispersed, and I was on my own running up a road. Finally I found Sam, behind all these police and riot shields round a corner. We went to another bar, our adrenalin up. I don't know if it was that, or because we were English and I had a New York Giants t-shirt on, but suddenly these girls were paying us loads of attention. Of course their boyfriends didn't much like it. It got a little bit heated. The guy behind the bar started to threaten us, with a handgun. So we did the off from this bar a bit sharpish. Then back in the hotel we thought, "Fuck this, we're English, we aint having this." So we went back. Having been warned off, warned to get out of this bar by a madman with a gun. We were all right. We had a laugh, me and Sam. We bonded.

America was good fun, and we were taken to some amazing places. To me they were amazing because they were big and glitzy. I was discovering different things, even down to the sandwiches. At Skyline Studios they asked us if we wanted to order some food in.

Oh yeah, you can have anything; you can order anything in, from anywhere, at any time. What do you want? Sushi? It was all so new to us. It was mad! They were all saying, "I'm gonna get the tuna melt, do you want the tuna melt?" I had no idea what that was. It's a sandwich with tuna, and melted cheese. I thought it sounded minging! Why would you do that? But we gave it a go. And yay, it's a tuna melt! I came home and made tuna melts. It's pathetic, but you didn't get sandwiches like that in the UK at the time.

Growing up in the East End, you did eat salt beef, bagels and all of that Jewish deli stuff. I was brought up on it and thought it was great. Suddenly I was where it came from. I was a bit ignorant about it. We were taken to the Carnegie Deli, to have their monstrous salt beef sandwiches, that are so big you can't even eat them, so big you have to take half home with you to eat on the plane. I wanted to know what real salt beef was. At home we have salt beef, and we have corned beef. But at home corned beef comes in a tin. What they call corned beef we would call salt beef. It's exactly the same. Pastrami is just different spicing. I'd only had pastrami sliced, cold out of packets in England. I didn't like it. I liked the idea of it and the sound of it. But I didn't like it. Out there I was suddenly eating real pastrami. I remember it well, I was taking an interest. But it was subliminal, I wasn't deliberately setting out to go the deli route and taste everything. But I was really a bit captivated by it all. I suppose because it related to my youth, both eating it, and then in the butcher's as well, learning to make it. I had a real interest in delis, especially when I was with Sam, we both loved all that.

"Me and Ray thought we'd open a deli one day. Well of course we were going to have houses in every country, and we were going to have a boat. But we also wanted to open a club, or a bar, a bit like a speakeasy, full of musicians. I always thought it would be really cool to have a bar like that, with live music, so if you wanted you could get up and jam. And it would be a restaurant too, doing great food that I'd cook. That's what I always thought about doing."

REUBEN

SALT BEEF TAKES ME BACK TO WHEN I WORKED IN THE
BUTCHER'S, AND EATING BAGELS AS A KID IN THE EAST END.
WHEN I WAS IN NEW YORK I TASTED THE REAL THING.
THIS DISH IS MY TAKE ON THE CLASSIC REUBEN SANDWICH

Ingredients: serves 6

Spice mix

1/2 tsp saltpetre - optional
60g rock salt
10g crushed black peppercorns
15g crushed allspice berries
15g crushed juniper berries
3 ground cloves
5g ground coriander seeds
5g ground chili flakes
3g ground caraway
5g ground cumin

45g black treacle
1 feather blade of beef, trimmed
    of any excess fat or gristle
300ml of beef stock or water

Pickled cucumbers

6 baby cucumbers
25g fine sea salt
250ml white wine vinegar
200g golden caster sugar
pinch of ground cloves
pinch of ground ginger
10g yellow mustard seeds

Pickled cabbage

60g coarse sea salt
1 white cabbage, finely shredded
1 litre white wine vinegar
45g sugar
1 star anise
1/2 stick of cinnamon
3 green cardamom pods
6 black peppercorns
3g coriander seeds
3g fennel seeds
3 juniper berries
1/4 grated nutmeg
1 large sprig of thyme
1 bay leaf
1 crushed clove of garlic

Onion purée

2 Spanish onions, peeled and
    finely sliced
a splash of olive oil
5g fine sea salt
3g caraway seeds
2tbsp crème fraîche

1 small cooked beetroot, cut
    into cubes
a few shavings of Emmental cheese
fresh horseradish root
a small handful of watercress

Rub the spice mix and treacle all over the beef, Put it into a plastic bag or clean container and chill it in the fridge for 5 days.

To make the pickled cucumbers, prick the cucumbers all over with a fork and cut in half lengthways. Lay them in a single layer in a non-reactive container, sprinkle with the salt and leave for a few hours.

Bring the rest of the pickling ingredients to the boil and simmer for a couple of minutes. Rinse the salt off the cucumbers then add them to the pickling liquor. Leave to cool then store them in the fridge.

To make the pickled cabbage, toss the salt thoroughly through the shredded cabbage. Put it into a plastic container, cover with parchment paper and place a weight on top. Chill it in the fridge for 1 week.

Remove from the fridge and rinse thoroughly under cold water to remove all the salt. In a non-reactive pan, bring the rest of the pickling ingredients to the boil, add the cabbage and simmer for 5 minutes. Once cool store it in the fridge. This will give you more than you need but it keeps for ages.

To cook the beef, put the feather blade into the pot of a pressure cooker along with 300ml of stock or water. Seal the lid and cook at full pressure for 35 minutes. Once cool, release the pressure and keep warm.

To make the onion purée, sweat the onions in the olive oil. Add the salt and caraway seeds and continue to sweat for at least 25 minutes or until very soft. Make sure you don't get any colour on the onions as we want to end up with a white purée.

Add the crème fraîche, continue to cook for a couple of minutes before transferring to a blender. Blitz until very smooth then push through a fine sieve. Keep warm, or chill it in the fridge, and gently reheat when needed.

To serve, spread a little of the warm onion purée on each plate. Carve the beef into six thick slices and place on the purée. Put a few cubes of beetroot on each piece of beef along with a few strands of pickled cabbage and some shavings of cheese. Grate a little fresh horseradish on top then place a pickled cucumber alongside each piece of beef. Garnish with watercress.

STAR-POWER

THAT ALBUM TOOK THREE-
AND-A-HALF YEARS AND COST A
MILLION QUID TO MAKE

We did a lot with Tony Taverner, who had worked with artists as diverse as Jeff Beck and Wham! Tony was great, his first question to the band was what football team do you support? He was studio manager at Maison Rouge in Fulham, so we were going to record at Maison Rouge, which was a legendary studio back then. Tony loved his grub, we used to have fun working out where we were going to eat. We'd drive to Wandsworth to make it to a pie and mash shop before closing. He used to call me the good grub geezer.

We spent months and months in Maison Rouge doing the album. We used to go for a break, have a couple of beers, or giggle juice, as Tony used to call it. We'd have a couple of pints, go back to the studio and always fall about laughing, pissed basically. I thought I could play pissed. I don't know now.

But we had a good time there, a good laugh. There are so many stories in that studio. In the early days the Blondes were signed to Queen's production team, so we used to bump into them a fair bit, and I had met Brian May. When we were recording in Maison Rouge, Queen were in the next room recording, so we got chatting. I talked a lot to Roger Taylor. There was a bar in Maison Rouge, and everybody hung out there. It was gated out front so there were no press or anything. It was really secret, and anything could go on. There was a TV room and table football, which Tony is the master at. He beats everybody. We all played each other, whatever bands were in. I always remember standing there and taking the piss out of Queen. Freddie Mercury came past us all and walked to the toilet. I needed to go for a piss as well, but said I wasn't going in there while Freddie was there. Everyone round the table went silent and Tony was staring at me, as Freddie was standing right behind me.

Freddie just said, "Don't flatter yourself, you should be so lucky, dear," and walked off. I'd met the rest of the band but never met Freddie. He was cool actually, he was all right.

Brian May started seeing Anita Dobson, who was huge in EastEnders at the time. So he would bring her to Maison Rouge because it was behind closed doors. They always used to eat at the Blue Elephant, a big Thai place bang opposite, and then come along to the studio where we would all be in the bar. And 'Ange' would moan about the bloody press, they would sit there opening the papers to a double spread on Den and Angie, and then leave it open on the bar. Brian May talked to Tony and had a listen to what we were up to.

It was just fun being in that environment all the time, in that studio, with the amount of people that either popped by or were working on a daily basis. One day the Fine Young Cannibals were in the studio. Then they left and went and recorded at the Town House. The record company told us they actually asked to transfer studios because they felt threatened by us. Because Tony was the studio manager I suppose we did practically live there. They probably saw us as a bit laddish, drinking and having a laugh. Five Star were in there a lot at the start with us too. Do you remember them? The five kids that wanted to be the English Jacksons.

A band Bill Drummond managed called Zodiac Mindwarp and the Love Reaction were around at that time. I did some vocals for them, with Ray and Nick, on one of their albums. The first single from it made the top ten, so reaching the heights for me.

There was a band on our record label at the time called Air Race, Sam knew the singer really well, Keith. And the drummer was Jason Bonham, son of the late John Bonham from Led Zeppelin.

"John Bonham is a rock god, a dead rock god, and my hero and inspiration."

There had been a Queen tour slot going and Air Race had done it, although it didn't go too well for them by all accounts. We were a bit pissed off that we had missed out on that, but then we were offered Fleetwood Mac. They had a few big shows at Wembley Stadium and we were going to do that. Obviously Harvey Goldsmith was the agent for Queen and Fleetwood Mac. But the buy-on was fifty grand a gig, which was mental back then. And they wouldn't even truck our equipment for that. Think how much money we were spending, we didn't care, our policy was to live in the Sunset Marquis, take a limo a hundred yards! My attitude was, so we've spent millions of pounds already, there will be millions more.

From the day I started in the Blondes, the day I gave up work, which was the biggest decision, I never had any doubt from that day on that I would be successful. I believed that self-doubt was not an option. The minute you start thinking of a contingency plan then you may as well stop, because then it won't happen. I'm not sure I necessarily believe that now but that was my thought process at the time.

I worked a lot as an extra on film and TV too, and that helped keep me going. And it was fun. A friend of mine, Gary Holton, who found fame playing Wayne in Auf Wiedersehen Pet, introduced me to his agent, and I got on their books. I've lost track of all the filming I did. I was in Only Fools and Horses, House of Cards, Between the Lines, Eastenders. And there were lots of films. I was in a movie called Hearts of Fire with Bob Dylan, which was filmed at The Electric Ballroom in Camden. When Barry Norman did a piece about it on TV the footage was all me, having a fight with Dylan from the front of the audience. I cottoned on to the fact that if I had an Equity card I could get category one or speaking parts, which paid more.

And because I had so much recorded stuff I qualified. I was always the down-and-out or vagrant. In The Bill I played a druggie who called for a doctor for his sick girlfriend, and because we were dossing down by the bins, I ran out and accosted the doctor for his medical bag when he arrived. I had to be all strapped up for that as the doctor grabbed it back and whacked me in the bollocks with it!

But I never had any money. There were times when it was my turn for a round in the pub and I didn't have the price of a pint. That was just the way it was. I didn't worry about it too much. And we had spent a bomb, we weren't even thinking of the costs. It did get crazy while we were at Maison Rouge. Ray lived in Cheshunt and I lived in Chingford, Nick was doing session work with us and he lived near Gatwick. Terry was in Queen's Park. Sam was either in Dulwich or near Peckham. So we were all very scattered. They gave us a cab account, so we would take cabs in and get a cab home, get a cab here, get a cab there. And then at weekends we weren't working, because of course working with Tony, Saturday is for football. Terry would take his family to Fulham to the swimming baths, and get a cab, or go shopping, and get a cab. I'd get cabs out to the West End. I'd be out at the St Moritz club at night, DJing for money, and get a cab back to Chingford. Then one day the record company turned round and said we had to address the cab account. They said we were spending three-and-a-half grand a week on taxis, in 1986!

They stopped the cab account, and we didn't know how we were going to get to the studio. A normal person would have used the fucking train, or bus, like I do now. They said that Ray lived the furthest, that Ray and me could come in together, but that was too expensive for a cab.

So they decided to put us up in a hotel in Marble Arch, in the Cumberland! Record company logic. We wanted to know how we were going to get from Marble Arch to Fulham Broadway? We could get cabs from there, that was okay. They should have said get a bus, get a life. Nick had to transport all his keyboards and stuff backwards and forwards, because he was a session player and didn't leave his stuff, as he was doing other work. So he got a hire car instead of a cab. Terry and Sam were close enough to keep their accounts. I think their attempt to reduce our three-and-a-half grand cab bill backfired.

You can have so much fun with it. But also you get a bit affected. You get a bit arsey. I know the movie Spinal Tap line for line. There's a bit where they are backstage and Nigel Tufnel is really going into one about the bread, he is complaining about the size of the bread and the meat, that you can't make a sandwich. It's quite funny and pathetic. I've been there and done that.

As a result of all of that the cost was racking up, but no one was telling us about it. I wasn't stupid, I was business-savvy enough to know that whatever we spent had to be recouped, and we would probably have to sell a shit-load of records to recoup all of it. But in those days if you sold lots of records you made lots of money and I thought we would. And what if we didn't make any money? We could work really hard, have a miserable existence and be unsuccessful at the end of it, have nothing out of it, not even a good experience. Or we could spend a million quid, which is fun. But the Fleetwood Mac dates cost too much money. I was a bit gutted because I was up for it. We all wanted to get out and do something.

Then finally a tour came up, Roger Taylor was doing a spin-off band called The Cross and he had released an album. They were doing a European tour and they wanted us. The beauty of it was, that although it was a different band, it wasn't Queen, it was still Roger Taylor from Queen. And he was using all of Queen's equipment, the same trucking, the people, the keyboard player. We were chuffed, we thought we would have a bit of a laugh, and use it as a warm-up to the release of the album. We had a great tour, it went really well. What we didn't realise was that Roger, after a couple of nights of watching us go down really well, tried to get us chucked off the tour in typical Spinal Tap fashion. The soundman that Sam knew told us. But they looked after us, the crew looked after us. We did the whole tour and had some good experiences.

We got to the final gig, in London, it was at the Town and Country, which is The Forum now I think, and the end of tour party was afterwards upstairs. Brian May was there. Jackie had come, and for years she'd been going on about how Brian May had been her teacher at school. I was chatting to Brian and asked him to do me a favour. I told him that for years my missus had been banging on about him being her teacher, and would he go over and say hello, because she still called him Mr May. It bugged me that, Mr May. I thought I had set her up, but over walks Brian and not only did he remember her, he knew her classmates' names. She was in her element. That was pretty cool, for him not only to come over and to say hi, but remember the people in her class.

"We were going to do the rest of the European tour, go to Germany and that, but we didn't. Partly because Roger didn't want us to I think, and we had bigger stuff to do. The record company wanted us to do a video with Nigel Dick, who was a great director, for our song When the World Cried, which was about John Lennon's shooting."

NIGEL WAS BASED IN LA
SO WE FLEW OUT THERE

"It was Sam's first time in LA, and we stayed in a small place around the corner from Sunset."

The hotel had a little swimming pool and a jacuzzi on the roof overlooking the Hollywood Hills. Beautiful. Nigel turned up to meet us as we arrived. He's a great guy, English, he used to be a musician on Stiff Records. He's done everything. We went out to dinner with our manager, and the record company. I don't remember what the restaurant was, I was so fucked by this time, it was late at night. I can just remember sitting there and then I actually went face down in a plate of food, I fell asleep at the table.

They picked us up early the next day and we went to do the video shoot. We had a great big Winnebago, with wardrobe and make-up at one end and a chill-out bit at the other. They had just wrapped filming with Guns N' Roses, the Sweet Child of Mine video. Nigel is in that film; you see a guy putting Slash's hat on, that's Nigel, the video director. The wardrobe girl was a little bit apprehensive about us. We found out that the day before, when they were doing Guns N' Roses' make-up in the van, Slash decided to sit in the front of the Winnebago and drive madly round the car park. But they said we were nice boys, because Axl was an utter wanker and Slash was driving the truck around. So we were a different kettle of fish. We were just pleased to be there I think.

I can remember we filmed all day, it got to about half ten at night and we ordered in a load of pizzas. I remember standing in this warehouse in the dark eating pizza. We didn't have any rock star moments about the size of the bread or anything.

The video was absolutely brilliant, it was quite arty. It had performance shots in that warehouse and then we went to downtown LA, under the bridge, the bridge that the Chili Peppers wrote about. We filmed all round seedy parts of town, it was supposed to look a bit New Yorky.

Nigel had a yellow taxi under the bridge with a taxi driver sitting there, and he had people mouthing little bits of the lyrics, about what it meant to them. You know how everyone remembers where they were when Kennedy got shot, this was meant to be the same thing about Lennon getting shot. It had all different people from all walks of life, and they auditioned all these actors. It was great, it looked like a movie, and all interspersed with the performance stuff.

When we came back to England the record company decided it was too depressing. Well, it's a fucking depressing song. It's about a tragedy, it's when the world cried. It's like Don McLean's American Pie, the day the music died.

Nigel got the right hump in America, so he made another video to shut the record company up, but he was taking the piss. He suggested he could get a couple of birds in, make them up to look like the girl on the album cover, and make them paint lyrics on a wall. The record company went for it, and that's the video. There isn't a copy of the original in existence, because it was never edited.

There is a girl on the album cover, with a tuning fork in her mouth. When we did our album design, Terence Donovan had just done the Robert Palmer video, Addicted to Love. I loved everything about it, and it made the song. And I thought it was an incredible video, the whole feel of it. We wanted a girl with that sort of look, and the tuning fork thing represented the Y, for Ya Ya. And it looked cool. So we got to sit in a studio in Clerkenwell and audition about 30 girls for that. They all had to come in, get undressed, have their hair slicked back, get made up and come out for us, no top on. We picked one, and then went for a beer. That was a day's work for me back in those days.

SOVIET-ERA

THE SINGLE WENT INTO THE CHARTS

"The record company didn't expect the single to sell like it did. They hadn't sorted out the distribution properly. So it charted and then dropped."

I remember being in Charing Cross Road, taking the phone call in a phone box when it went into the charts. We went to the St Moritz Club and emptied them of champagne. Then the Sunday came and it had dropped out because no one could actually buy it. Bit gutting.

We needed to tour, to play, and our lousy UK representation came up with a Russian tour through a Polish promoter he knew. Perestroika was happening, Gorbachev and Reagan were in the news. Very few Western acts had been out there, and if they had they'd only done Moscow or Leningrad. They said they were going to do a lot of filming, and that we would have the rights. We thought that would look cracking for the next video, and it was exciting, to go somewhere like that.

The record company was totally against it; they said they had plans around the album release. But when we pushed them they wouldn't tell us what. So we just thought, "Bollocks to you, we're going to go." We told the promoter we'd go but could only do a couple of weeks, partly because Nick was up for it but as a session musician he had commitments.

The first shows were in Kiev and when we got there they took us to check our equipment, meet the road crew, and see the venue. It was a fantastic 12,000-seat stadium. Our gear was being unloaded on stage, and they were pulling t-shirts out, merchandise. Tour t-shirts! I opened up this Ya Ya t-shirt, and it had all the tour dates on the back. There were 60 odd dates on the back of this shirt.

Sixty gigs. Three-and-a-half-months. Mental. Nick went mad because he had to get back. We had a big meeting, the UK rep Bernie had stitched us up. We set about him in a bar, I literally had to pull Nick off him.

They had taken our passports away, we were threatening to go home, but couldn't. There were contracts. And back then you could barely make a phone call home, you had to book it in advance and then you were being listened to. We had a KGB representative with us the whole time, listening, and any kids hanging around us would be taken away for questioning.

We started the tour with a lot of bad blood. We played seven republics. I've got a photo of us all at the start backstage and I've got a photo of us all exactly the same backstage three-and-a-half months later, about three-and-a-half stone lighter. The smallest gig was about a 10,000-seater. In Moscow alone we did 10 or 12 shows, in succession, in a 12,000-seater.

And there were no filming days, no footage, nothing.

Out there for that amount of time you start to lose the plot a little bit. It wasn't like we could go into a bar and get a coffee, you couldn't get anything anywhere. You couldn't even get drinkable water, and food was non-existent.

I had thousands of roubles in the end, I gave them away. What can you buy with roubles? We found an old department store with a football in the window and thought we'd have a kick around. We queued for hours just to be told there weren't any. In the end all we could buy were records of Lenin's favourite songs and things like that. So we were all wandering around the streets with balalaikas and Lenin memorabilia.

They took us to see so many churches and icons. I hate churches. None of us were interested. Show us a bar.

In Kiev even when we went back to the hotel there were all these priests in their long robes in the lobby. Looking closer we saw that one of them was Robert Runcie. The Archbishop of Canterbury was on a state visit, and he had all these people around him dressed in long, flowing purple robes. We got chatting, and told him we were a band from London, on tour. He invited us to join him when he took tea in his room, at 3 o'clock. It was almost like an official engagement. We all got changed and traipsed off to Robert Runcie's suite, then sat around and had a chat. At one point I remember a noise and looking around, a guy came out the bathroom in all of his robes; he had obviously been having a shave, and he had all bits of tissue stuck over his face where he'd cut himself shaving. It was so surreal. And I remember Runcie saying, "Who is going to be Mum?" and pouring the tea. We talked about his wife, who is apparently a brilliant musician. He invited us to Lambeth Palace where he was living, any time we were in London. He said, "Come by and have tea at the Palace because my wife would love it. She's a brilliant piano player." I had visions of us all around a piano with his missus, Chas and Dave style.

Tour madness set in, and I don't think drink helps. There was no water and they were smuggling us in pure Siberian vodka.

In the mornings we'd wake up and brown slime would come out the taps, or nothing, just thumping pipes and sand. So what are you going to brush your teeth in, because the water was giving everyone the shits and making us ill? The vodka was much cleaner, so I used to brush my teeth with vodka. And that gives you the taste, doesn't it?

We got to Moscow eventually, there were lots of soldiers in the audience, as always on that tour. They were only kids really. They'd try and smuggle things in to give us; a hat or whatever.

So we started collecting military hats and then even Russian uniforms. They must have been risking their lives. We had air force ones and military ones. I'd never get in them now, you should see how small they are.

I remember on my birthday, going on stage in Moscow and 12,000 people singing Happy Birthday, which was quite cool. And then backstage we had an interview with a national newspaper. Being rebellious, we all put our uniforms and dark glasses on and sat in a line, and would only say, "Niet, niet" to everything the interviewer asked.

Later, on a plane, there was a guy reading the paper and looking over his shoulder at me. And there was our picture. Terry asked him to translate it, and it said we had been in the country too long and had lost the plot!

We were on our way to Armenia, we'd heard a rumour there was a war going on, but they lied to us and said it was fine. Then we were met by military in Jeeps at an airfield completely surrounded by barbed wire. They took us to this hotel, and all the windows and doors were boarded up, though they unlocked it for us. We checked in, and then they opened up the bar. We met the chef, who was going to be cooking for us specially. It turned out all he could say and all he could cook was shashlik, which was great, as at least we were getting meat.

So we were in this war zone, and there was a military coup going on.

There was a massive arena, about 10,000 seats. The military were always at the front anyway, security and soldiers had the best seats, but this was like a sea of soldiers. They loved it, it was a brilliant gig.

Every now and again the Polish promoter would book a restaurant, one of the private underground places.

"There would always be borscht with beef, which was usually beetroot-based."

There were really amazing broths, they explained stocks to me, the long, slow, simmering of bones. I went through a phase after that of putting beetroot in my stocks to make them brown and rich, I don't do it any more because it makes them all taste the same. But that combination of beef and beetroot is a really good one, and I do love beetroot.

When I was a kid in the East End, we used to buy jars of a horseradish from the Jewish section in the supermarket. A creamed horseradish, but with beetroot. I've made it since, blitzed up beetroot, horseradish, and crème fraîche and put it on salt beef sandwiches. I recognised that in Russia.

And the other thing was the caviar. When I was a kid my Dad sometimes went to Denmark for work, and every year they sent us a Christmas hamper, with all kinds of weird things in it, tins of things that as a kid you're not really into. And it always had a tin of caviar. No one liked it so it used to sit in the fridge for years. Then in Russia they brought out some proper Beluga over ice, little tiny eggs, black-gold in colour, that they'd serve with dark brown rye bread and shots of pure iced vodka. And I tell you, I've never had it like that since, and probably never will again.

There were things that were humbling about that tour. I can remember standing in the street, and there were hundreds of little kids. They were all Pioneers, part of the baby communists movement. They say it's their equivalent of the Cubs or the Scouts. But it's very military, they're all in their little uniforms and their Thunderbirds hats and they've got their Pioneer badges. I didn't have kids then, but I still thought they were really cool. They were all very polite and probably spoke an average of seven languages!

They chatted to us and gave us their Pioneer salute. They gave me my own Pioneer badge, which I've still got. They had so little and made so much effort.

But for the most part the long stay got really tedious. I kept losing my temper and I'd kick off. And Ray was always having problems because he couldn't phone home, he was missing his girlfriend. He put his fist through a big double glass door on the hotel floor; he punched it in a temper. That meant we had to miss a couple of gigs because he was all bandaged up and couldn't play. When you're in a band your release is on stage at night, if there's no show or you can't play you've got no energy release. That's when the problems start. Every time there's not a show it ends up in a piss-up and then trouble.

I wanted to go home; I wanted to have a proper cooked dinner; to be able to cook something myself. So some lovely old Russian people that didn't speak any English let me come and stay with them. They lived in a cooperative block, which is like a council estate really, in the middle of nowhere in Riga. They were the parents of some fans we got close to, because they had come to lots of the gigs. So I ended up staying in a little single flea-bitten room in their place, with a tiny little kitchen with ants crawling about. I remember them making me roast chicken. They probably had to queue up for all this stuff for days. We had a whole roast chicken and I sat and ate it, like a family meal, with two people that didn't speak English.

"I stayed there for a few days. The band thought I'd gone off my head. But I needed space. I was just sleeping and recharging because I'd been partying and drinking like a fish. I can remember the bed, the kitchen and the chicken. I don't remember anything else. I couldn't even tell you if I was there for two days or a week."

i RECKON i HAD A BiT
OF A MELTDOWN

BEETROOT-CHEESECAKE

Ingredients: serves 8

1/2 large onion, peeled and
     chopped
a knob of butter
500g cooked beetroot, diced
1 tsp orange zest
juice of 1 orange
8g ground caraway
10g Forum Cabernet Sauvignon
     vinegar
5g fine sea salt
a few grinds of white pepper
3 leaves gelatine, soaked in cold
     water to bloom
250g oatcakes
100g butter, melted
200g Philadelphia full fat
     cream cheese
3 egg whites

To make the cheesecake, sweat the onion in
the butter until soft and translucent. Add the
beetroot, orange zest and juice, caraway, vinegar,
salt and pepper. Cover and simmer for 5 minutes.
Transfer to a blender then add the gelatine.
Purée until smooth. Leave to drain through muslin.

In a food processor, blitz the oatcakes with
the melted butter. Spread over the base of a
springform tin, pressing firmly. Place it in the
fridge to set.

Beat the cream cheese into the drained purée.
Whisk the egg whites until they hold soft peaks,
then fold into the mixture.

Spread evenly over the biscuit base then chill
it in the fridge again. Once set, gently warm the
drained juices and pour them over the
cheesecake to glaze. Chill it in the fridge once
more until required.

To serve, use a warm wet knife to cut it.

We serve this with pickled and roast beetroot,
horseradish, crème fraîche and nasturtium
leaves at The West House.

YOU CAN JUST HAVE THE CHEESECAKE, OR SERVE IT WITH
DIFFERENT BITS OF BEETROOT, PICKLED, ROAST, A PUREE,
LOTS OF DIFFERENT COLOURS. THIS IS A MEETING OF RUSSIAN
BEETROOT WITH JEWISH DELI CHEESECAKE

SESSIONS-AND BABY-FOOD

WHEN YOU COME OFF A TOUR
iT'S AN ANTICLIMAX

> "I'd been chased by mobs clamouring for us, and played massive venues every night in Russia for three-and-a-half months."

When I got home I'd stick the telly on and there was Billy Joel live in Leningrad. I've played there, in the same stadium.

So when you come back you can get into a weird frame of mind. It's so exciting seeing people again, until you're back, because that euphoria you were expecting doesn't really exist. The thought of coming back and seeing people is much better and stronger than the reality. Terry used to equate it with being an astronaut. He wondered what it would have been like to be Buzz Aldrin or Neil Armstrong, going up there and coming back. I used to say, "We've been on tour Terry, we haven't been to the fucking moon." But everybody else is not part of what you've done, so it's always a real anticlimax. All of a sudden I was at home and with no release for this adrenalin.

Because we'd been a bit cut off out there, we didn't really know what was happening with the record companies and promotion. They hadn't wanted us to go. We were also supposed to have gone to America to promote the album and single. That hadn't happened as a result of our absence. But we came back thinking, "Well, we're shit hot right now." We were well rehearsed, we'd just done 60-plus shows. We were as tight as, we were the best we were ever going to be.

But we came back to nothing, it had all gone a bit cold. We started doing demos and working for the next album, but got a cold response, until the record company had no interest at all.

The irony is that a couple of years ago, Ray, the guitar player, was working in a music shop in Melton Mowbray where he lives now. One of the reps came into the shop when Ray was on his laptop in the office, burning a few Ya Ya tracks. This rep saw him and said, "Fucking hell! I love that album.

"I've been trying to get hold of a copy for so long for my missus, it was always her favourite album." The guy used to be a record plugger for Warner Brothers. They got talking and he wanted to know what had happened. Ray told him about the Russian tour. This guy said that when he was working for Warners, they had Top of the Pops lined up for us, and all this big TV, loads of stuff. It was all good to go. There was going to be a massive push on us, and we went to Russia, and got stuck there. So you suddenly realise that on the turn of a coin, it would have been a completely different situation. But you can say that about so many things.

Terry was the first one that went and got a proper job, and I just thought that was the beginning of the end really. Then Ray was growing apart because of his girlfriend and the people he was hanging around with. He was playing little pub gigs in his band, Lend Us a Quid, which was a covers band. And he kept moving further and further away.

Sam is a bit of a worker. He started doing sessions. Zodiac Mindwarp and the Love Reaction had just come back from their American tour with Guns N' Roses, and the guitarist and bass player were forming a band on their own. Me and Sam got together with them and cut some demos. They were absolutely brilliant, to be honest. They were quite ahead of what was going on at the time. I think we could have just taken them to Warner Brothers and it would have been good. But then things went wrong. They wanted a scream-and-shout singer. Sam went off to do his own thing. It just all kind of drifted apart. I started doing sessions and I had a really bad time of it. If I don't get the music, I just can't get into to it.

"I must have been with Jackie for about nine years by then. I'd known her for about 10, and lived with her for about nine. I don't do marriage, or even other people's weddings. I don't send engagement cards. I think it's tosh. You meet someone, you get on and you do what you do. We're partners, but we were always like friends, mates."

WE DECIDED TO HAVE KIDS

"Jake was born on Christmas Eve in '91, and Jess in October '93."

Jake was born the year that we moved to the house in Chingford. I was still poncing about somehow. I was recording, still writing for movies and stuff, some of which got used. We still had the same manager in America, who was trying to get us bits. We had a room at home set up like a studio. Then Jake was born and he had his cot in there. I remember him having guitar amps and that under the cot.

It was a couple of years of not really working for a living, sitting around the house and cooking a lot, watching cookery programmes.

Jackie would go off to work and I'd look after Jake and take him down to the clinic, cook, and then she'd come home from work to relieve me of my duties. Not such a hard day! He was pretty easygoing. I took him down to the pub sometimes when it was sunny, to their little beer garden, had a couple of beers and sat with him in his pushchair, read the paper. The people in the baby-weighing clinic asked me if I would come and do a talk to the young mums about how to feed the baby. Jake was getting bigger and bigger. I used to purée everything for him.

I was so into cooking when I was at home. I'm not a DIY man. I hate DIY. My Dad's done it all his life. My house always smelled of paint when I was a kid. You'd go home and the wallpaper was changed. They were always decorating. It drove me mad. But I did do our kitchen, that's important. I cut a hole in the floor and dug out the foundations, and we laid two RSJs, with concrete and bricks underneath to build a plinth to take an Aga. This kitchen was tiny, and I put an Aga in there! It cost a load of money. I remember getting a loan on the mortgage and we got a bit extra to do the kitchen up and I went out and I bought it.

I got all this stuff. I wanted to be a chef.

I remember making a pizza. When should babies start eating solid food?

Jackie came home and Jake was covered in tomato sauce, he was in his high chair and he had his bib on and there was tomato sauce all round his mouth and face, all in the high chair and everywhere, probably on me as well. But he was enjoying it because he was sat up there with me, trying to make the dough and roll it out, then making tomato sauce. That's all it had, and a bit of mozzarella, a bit of basil, nothing major. That was his first solid food, he was six or seven months old.

But I was getting bored, I couldn't go and do sessions and leave him.

I went to see a friend that had a pub in Covent Garden called the Maple Leaf, a big Canadian pub in Maiden Lane next door to Rules, which is the oldest restaurant in London. I'd always mucked around cooking with her and we'd gone to restaurants together. She was trying to sort out her menu at the pub. She asked me if I'd go in and help. I went, not that I knew what I was doing. They assumed I did for some reason.

I went down to their kitchen, spent a day reorganising, and did a bit of work behind the bar. The chef from Rules, Neil Pass, came in on his break for a sandwich or whatever. So I met him and he said that if I ever wanted to see what a real kitchen was like, I could come down and do a service. So that's what I did. He put me on the fish with a Vietnamese guy, who didn't speak very much English, and if he did I didn't understand him. I didn't know how kitchens worked. It was huge and suddenly lunch kicked in and I didn't know what was going on. God, we were in the shit! There was fish everywhere, we were opening oysters and the orders were being called over a tannoy that we couldn't hear. We had a couple of hundred for lunch. At the end of service, Neil asked me if I had enjoyed it. I didn't think it was really cooking, it was just mental. But he said he thought I did really well, that I should definitely pursue it.

There was one chef, a guy called Kevin Hopgood, who had really long hair like I did. He was soft-spoken, and he kept asking the other chefs to save him a bit of what they were prepping. He wanted to taste their things and wasn't on that night. Out of everyone in the kitchen he was the only one talking about stuff and tasting stuff. He was really into his food and seemed very knowledgeable, and also a nice, mild-mannered guy. We're still mates to this day.

I phoned up straight away and thanked Neil for the opportunity, and then I went back to do an evening service. Working with the sous chef there I learned something about professional kitchens. I made a hollandaise with tarragon vinegar. There was a big mountain of it and it tasted nice, I'd seasoned it well. Then the sous chef tasted it and said it needed much more seasoning. I thought the result was horrendous. Then during the service, the chef got quite angry, shouting, "Who made this fucking hollandaise?" The sous chef blamed me, he stitched me up.

I had adverts from the back of cookery magazines, I wrote off to three major cookery schools for more information. I got a shock because they were thousands of pounds per term. I went to Neil Pass for advice. He said not to bother with those schools, that it would only cost a fortune. He gave me the phone number of a couple of agents and suggested I phone them up, register on their books and go and do casual work and learn like that. I didn't feel comfortable with that, I never used the numbers, it didn't feel right going into someone's kitchen as a casual, being paid but not really knowing what I was doing.

So I phoned Westminster and enrolled. I put my forms in, and got a place on day release, which meant that I had to be in employment. So I made out I was a chef at Rules.

TRAINEE CHEF

i BOUGHT all THE cHEF GEAR,
BECAUSE oBViOUSly i DiD;'T
HAVE woRK clOTHES

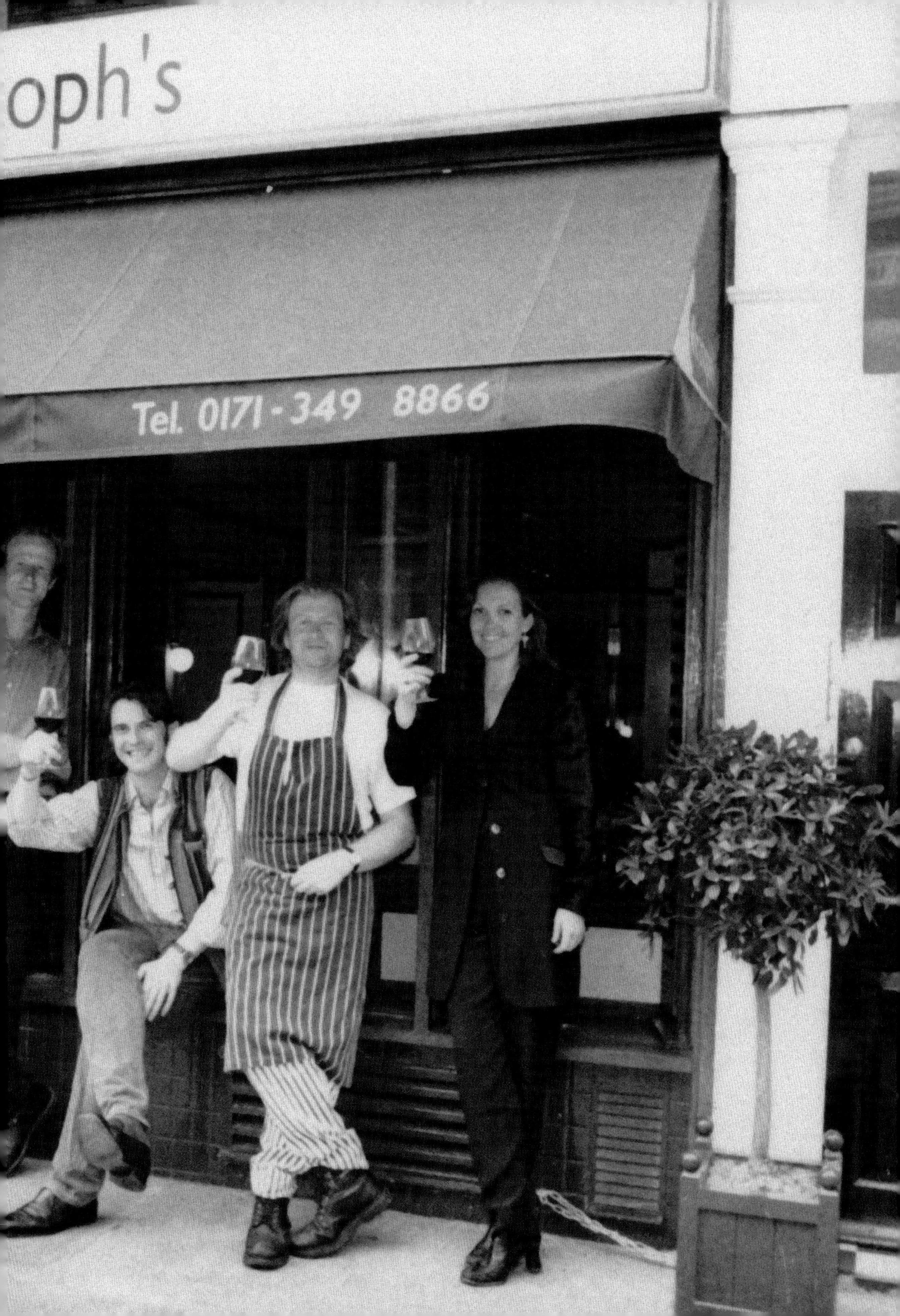
oph's
Tel. 0171-349 8866

> "Neil Pass said that if I was really adamant about training, Westminster College was the best, the only one worth going to."

I remember turning up there, going into the changing room and getting dressed in all this stuff I'd never worn before. I had checked trousers, a white jacket and this tourniquet thing you have to wear. I had no fucking idea what that was for. So in good 80s drumming tradition I rolled it up, and tied it round my head as a headband. I got screamed and shouted at, going into class. But we did a little bit of cooking and I got put into a reasonably good group. The teacher was one of the better ones, Kevin Selwood. I was doing all right, for one day a week I was quite enjoying it.

I had been there for around six weeks when I got called out to go and see Kevin in his office. Although I'd made out I was from Rules to get in I couldn't say I was still working there, because then they'd ask if I was practising at work, and some of the students were being paid for by their work. I didn't pay anything, I'd blagged it through the dole. Every week they'd ask if I had a job yet, and I said no.

So I thought I'd been rumbled, and he did ask me what my story was. I just came clean, and told him I wasn't really a chef but a musician. And then he told me that the reason they were calling me in was because one of the college lecturers was opening a restaurant in Holborn and wondered if I'd be interested in a job.

So I couldn't come back from that, could I?

They arranged for me to go and meet this lecturer, Vince Morse, who was opening Procter's in Holburn. I took the job. In the end we painted the outside, cleaned up the stoves, you name it, we did everything to get it open in time for Christmas '92.

In January '93 I started in proper full-time employment, I was working alongside Vince at the start. I thought he was brilliant because I'd never seen anything else. His menu was like the Eagle, which was the first real gastropub.

I used to love it in there, and that's what I wanted to do. It was very inspiring. So although Procter's was a brasserie in the West End, we wrote a blackboard menu, a new menu every day.

It was me, Vince, and then he hired some guy as his sous chef. When he left me with the sous chef I noticed the sous chef syndrome again, like I'd experienced at Rules. As soon as he'd gone out of the kitchen this guy started trying to do it his way, which just looked like something out of Harvester to me. I didn't like the fact that as soon as the chef walked out he started dissing him and changing the food, and cutting corners. I stood up to him one day, and he picked up a big knife and said, "You should have a bit more respect, my friend" and started waving it at me. I was a bit hot-headed and as soon as he started waving a knife at me I picked up a stool that had my chopping board on it and I threw the chopping board at him and then hit him with the stool to disarm him. This was in an open kitchen.

Mayhem had broken out in the restaurant, I was hauled off, we were separated. I got my coat. But they didn't do the disciplinary thing. They said they couldn't tolerate fighting or violence, however they understood that I was provoked and that I gave a shit and he didn't. So they sacked him and I stayed.

They brought in a head chef, Andy Ives, who Vince had worked with at Carriages. Andy was a lovely bloke, real old-school, hotel-trained, he could turn a mushroom in seconds, so he showed me a lot of classical things. He's the only man I know that can probably recite every potato garnish in the repertoire.

Andy and I used to do the menus together and we got to a point where he started to rely on me, we worked together well. I was being pushed, learning, if I didn't know something I'd whizz out to the office where Vince had all his books on the shelf and work something out. I was allowed to do my own dishes and as time went on I started doing more and more. I was doing the menus, then I was doing the costings, then I was doing everything on the computer, learning the ropes.

They made the decision to get rid of Andy, and it was awful, they did it at Christmas. He came back after New Year and they sat him down and told him he didn't have a job any more. He sorted himself out pretty quickly, but I was gutted and it never sat very comfortably.

They said that I was running the kitchen anyway, that if they didn't do something they were going to lose me, because I would want to progress and was clearly going places. So they were either going to lose me and keep him, or promote me. That was the only way forward. I did understand that, and carried on there and became head chef. Suddenly the pressure was different because the buck stopped with me. I really struggled with it because it was too soon for me. I was there three-and-half years in total, with about a year as head chef.

At Procter's I used to do a lot of smoking, curing meats myself. We made duck ham, cured lamb in boxes in ash. I've always made my own sausages, which stems back to making sausages when I was a kid in the butchers. We had beetroot-cured salmon with horseradish. It looked great and we really perfected it. I used to do mackerel with piccalilli and green beans. I kept the piccalilli sauce light with the cauliflower and blanched the green beans, and I put fresh almonds on it. Risotto has always been big for me, and that's where I perfected that too. Another thing was bread and butter pudding, bread and butter was the stand-by dessert.

Charles Campion used to come in a fair bit. After I was head chef I'd give him dishes from time to time for an opinion. Then one day out of the blue the phone rang and it was Charles. He said, "Hello, old boy. Just to let you know that if you get any weird and wonderful phone calls from various people, it's because I've put your name out there to a few people that are looking for soldiers at the moment." I thanked him and he said, "It's just that I think your cooking deserves a wider audience."

One of the calls was from a guy called Christoph Brooke, he was looking to find the next star chef. It turned out not only had they been in to check me out, he'd brought his shareholders and his Dad, three or four times in one week. They loved what they were eating and were opening a restaurant in Park Walk next to the Aubergine. I had to go for it. I told them at Procter's, they were quite happy for me. I helped them recruit a new chef, trained him, invited them to the opening, it was all good.

And I went off to Christoph's and it was fucking mayhem, it went mad! It was like walking back into a band. I had PR, I had everything. From the very short time we were open there I have a thick book of cuttings and reviews. Faye Maschler's restaurant openings of the year were me, an Irish guy called Richard Corrigan, and a new young guy called Heston Blumenthal at a pub called the Fat Duck.

The other two went on to do quite well, I don't know what fucking happened to me.

We got great reviews all round. We were open for 18 months, and it was very rock and roll. I was out of control though, I was really manic. I probably thought I had to be Ramsay, who was next door. I was an animal.

"There was a lot of pressure. I was older so could maybe handle things better than some youngsters in that position, but I wasn't ready for it. I wasn't an experienced enough cook. I really was in way above my head and yet being hailed in the press, and I thought, "I can't even cook." I was learning from everybody and everything. I still do."

"You can't ever stop learning about cooking. It evolves all the time."

We were the buzz, and Christoph was a bit of a party boy, so everyone came, you name it. And the pair of us were on the front of The Caterer before we even opened. Gordon Ramsay was always in, sitting on the freezer, munching his way through our mise en place. Or I'd sit in the Aubergine eating his petit fours and drinking his coffee. And Marcus Wareing was always with us.

Jennifer Sharp helped me quite a bit. She used to be the editor of Harper's & Queen. Amy Grub was her alias for the food columns. I remember when she first came and ate my food. I didn't know her, I didn't know she was in, I just knew there was some woman upstairs having a moan because we had hake on the menu and we'd run out. She demanded to see me after she'd eaten. I went up, and Ramsay was in as always. She started chatting, going on about the food. I was trying to be polite and then Ramsay started chipping in. She clearly didn't know who he was and he introduced himself as my sous chef. She was having a go at me and he was pissing around with his bullish charm. She got cross, told him it was rude to speak, and that she was trying to talk to his chef. His arms were sunburnt and she took the piss out of his sunburn. So he told her he'd been on a boat all week. She asked him what he'd been doing on a boat. And he said, "Trying to catch your fucking hake," which was a brilliant response and very funny.

When he left she said to me, "My God, what an obnoxious young man, don't you keep him in check and tell him how to behave?" I said, "He doesn't really work here, he's next door at the Aubergine, that's Gordon Ramsay." She went flying out of the restaurant after him.

The next morning she sent me a postcard and thanked me for an amazing meal.

I brought with me a lot of the things I had learnt at Procter's, like the charcuterie plate we always had on the menu. It would have seven or eight different things on it, a terrine, a salami. Now it's something you see a lot, but you didn't then. My idea in doing it was to be making all the charcuterie ourselves.

Having major PR, Jori White, there was always something going on. I did a screen test for Ready, Steady, Cook, where I had to cook from the blind bag. Then the production team said, "We've got this black guy who's really popular and always wins, the ladies love him, and it'd be really cool if maybe, because you used to play drums, if you could play pots and pans with some wooden spoons, and Ainsley can do a calypso dance." So, as I wasn't up for that, I think that might have been the end of my TV career there and then.

Coming from music, with its madness, I didn't like that whole side of things. I wanted to get my head down and be a serious cook. To make up for all those years lost, because I was so late coming to it.

I was running the show, based on bollocks, and trying to learn. I was completely and utterly out of control. But when you do have time to reflect you think, actually that's not that clever. You know, if you're bullied you're gonna be a bully, it's as simple as that. But you can make different choices.

There is a discipline required because you're dealing with knives and fire, and dodgy temperaments and the works. You're like a headmaster, teacher, agony aunt, alcohol and drugs counsellor, you name it. It's an environment that people don't understand unless they've been there.

"We had that one mental year of being the best new opening before it all died down and people moved on."

There were lots of shareholders, people wanting us to change stuff, and it wasn't really happening. We had a rough six months and the owners started looking at different options. And along came Nico.

Roy Ackerman's Restaurant Partnership had approached legendary chef Nico Ladenis to open loads of restaurants. Simply Nico in Victoria was trading as a bistro, and Nico Central had André Garrett as the chef at the time. Of course there was the big three-star Chez Nico, but they had done a deal to roll out these more casual Simplys and Centrals. Nico and Roy Ackerman were looking at lots of sites, came to have dinner at Christoph's, and thought it would be an ideal site.

In the kitchen it was manic, we had Nico in for dinner, God was coming to dinner! Everyone was scrubbed up, hats on and everything, down in the basement. Not that he came down or anything, but everyone made a real effort, it was a big deal. Anyway, we fed them and I got summoned to the table, and Nico asked me where I had worked before? He said my food was familiar to him, in its combinations and style. My Gastronomy is my bible, the combinations list in that book was my mantra. So that was interesting.

And although it's probably all bullshit and flannel like with a lot of these people, he said that it was probably one of the best meals out he'd ever had.

On reflection, what a load of bullshit! But at the time it was fantastic. He asked me to come by his office on Monday morning at 8 o'clock for a coffee. Fuck me, I'd been invited for coffee by Nico!

So I went and he said he was looking for restaurant sites, thinking of buying our Chelsea site, and changing it into a Nico restaurant. He wanted to know if I'd be interested in staying, he'd done his research and felt I had a very good following in the area, and that my food was fantastic.

They wanted me to head up Nico Chelsea. Why wouldn't I? I said I'd be more than happy to.

I farmed all my staff out into the various Nico operations to learn the ropes and to keep them employed. And I oversaw the building project while also going to work at all the existing restaurants, to see how they did things. I liked some of what I saw and hated some of what I saw, like you would.

My friend Kevin Hopgood, who was then at Elena's L'Etoile (of The Restaurant Partnership), had a little heart scare. His blood pressure was really high. He was signed off work for a bit, so I went and ran his kitchen as head chef for a few weeks with Elena Salvoni. Elena is the grand maître d' of Soho. She is the most famous restaurant maître d' in this country and utterly brilliant, she knows every customer by name.

And then we got Nico Chelsea open. The politest way of putting this: the whole organisation was a crock of shit. I didn't know it at the time, but I also needed to get out of London. I just wasn't happy.

I was approached by the guys that had set up Soho House. They had a project. They'd bought this big old country pile just outside of Frome, Babington House, to be their country outpost of Soho House. After a couple of meetings they took me down there with Jackie. We had a look at what was just a derelict house. They had plans to build a spa and were going to reinstate the Victorian walled garden to supply the kitchen. Monty Don was advising on the garden and Rose Gray's daughter was advising on a wood-burning oven to make pizzas.

They had all these great people, which was quite exciting for me, and I had lots of ideas for it too. So I cooked for them, I cooked at Soho House, and I spent time in Frome. I was into it and decided to do it, to up sticks and go.

They started looking for a house for me and the family down there. I looked at schools and spent some time in Somerset.

I had to tell Roy Ackerman and hand in my notice. We talked about my plans and they asked if I would be prepared to talk about staying. I said that I was committed to Babington House. They asked me to just talk to them about staying, and then offered me the post of executive chef over the whole group. They had lots of openings scheduled, and others in the offing, and I would get paid a bonus on each opening. They said I should go away, have a think, and write down anything I could think of I might want. I obviously wasn't meant to come back with a silly shopping list, but that is what I did. I didn't know what else to do really. I wrote pros and cons, but then I wrote down a shopping list of terrorist demands: helicopter, Swiss bank account. I just wrote down loads and loads of stuff. I felt I would need at least all of that to even consider staying.

They took the list, went away to have a talk, and came back with almost all of them ticked, at which point I didn't know what to do. Jackie and I talked about it, and realised that even if I just stayed in London and did it for one year, which was not the plan, it was still financially a no-brainer.

So I had to do the right thing and phone Soho House, people who I really got on with, and explain the situation. I was really sorry, and they were cool. They didn't think I was making the right move, but they understood.

It turns out the reason Ackerman said yes to everything on my shopping list was because it was an impossible job, and because they had no intention of honouring it. I could have put down that I wanted to be the Emperor of China and they would have ticked it.

Exec chef, fantastic! I had to set up and open every new restaurant, including being involved in the planning stages. They had no HR department, so I had to recruit staff, kit out, sort supplies, open, do menus, and set up everything for each new place, and be there and cook in each fucking restaurant. I had to do all of that, and if something went wrong, the buck stopped with me.

I wasn't on a great salary because I was going to get paid on each opening. They then decided that my salary couldn't come out of head office, I had to be on the payroll of each restaurant that I opened. And they were crap salaries as each was a new untried place. In theory I got a bonus for each opening, which I never saw. So I was working for a lousy basic salary, expected to run each new place and keep the standards up, as well as set up and run the next one and train the new head chef there. So I started taking my key brigade, my sous chef, with me to each opening, just to be sure I could do it.

I was driving from Chelsea to Heathrow on my motorbike, doing their service, and then back to Chelsea in time to put the rubbish out and make sure everything was done in Chelsea. Then on my way home I'd stop by the Barbican, every day. And then I opened London Bridge, which was a big one in London Bridge Hotel. I was stressed beyond belief, I was getting really depressed. It was just a completely undoable job situation. I hated it. It wasn't creative in any way, shape or form.

I remember I finally had a day off, and was asked to go the anniversary party of the Nico restaurant in Manchester. The great and the good of the city were going to be there at a big party. They wanted me in the kitchen. They had bought my ticket. I said I couldn't go, that I was knackered, and not the chef there anyhow. I was told that if I wasn't on the train from Euston the following day I didn't have a job.

I left work that night early, about 10:30, went home to Chingford, packed my bag, got my head down for a couple of hours, got up, got to Euston early in the morning, got a train to Manchester with the ticket they'd bought me. I got to Manchester, got in a taxi to the Midland Hotel, walked in, introduced myself to the chef. 9:00am I was in their kitchen, just stood there like a spare part, prepping like a casual, doing potatoes and stuff all day long for the dinner. I didn't even know what the menu was. A bottle of water was all I had all day, until the party ended, at about 11 o'clock. They gave me a room in the hotel, I went up, crashed out, got up in the morning, ate breakfast, and got the train back in time for the London Bridge lunch service.

So that was my life and I had no option. My plan then was to see my year out, so I could get paid my bonuses and go.

It got to Easter time, when it's dead in the city, with no one in the London Bridge Hotel. We had agreement to shut for the weekend. So my right-hand men, Phil and Barry, had bought their train tickets home. Then I got a phone call late the night before Good Friday. They had just had a company meeting and decided that we would open over the holiday. I protested and reminded them they had agreed to shutting. But they said they had decided and we would open. I thought it was pointless, but was told that it didn't matter what I thought. I told the boys to go, and went into a 90-cover restaurant in the middle of the city on my own and just opened the door, just to be there if the phone rang. It was dead. I just sat there with the door shut for most of Good Friday, but the boys got their time off.

I finally went away for a week and left Barry in charge. There was a guy front of house who'd been away at the same time. When he and I got back he looked around and saw Barry in the kitchen and kicked off about him being there.

Barry had left for a bit, but I explained he had come back while we were away. He said Barry should get out, I said he had helped us out and was back. In the end it got a bit heated and I told him that he should look after his staff and I'd look after mine. He said he was in charge of the whole thing. I was fuming, and he wouldn't calm down.

I said, "If he walks out the fucking door, I'm going with him." He said, "Fine." So I rolled my knives up, got my stuff, apologised to the other boys in the kitchen for dropping them in the shit, and Barry and I walked out.

I can remember driving to work one morning just before this happened, on my bike. I always used to feel like I was on borrowed time on a motorbike in London. I'd get home at night and I'd think, I've made it, especially if it was raining or snowing. Sometimes I'd stay at work and sleep in the restaurant. But there was one day I was driving to work. I was just coming over London Bridge, before the left turn down to where the restaurant was. I was looking at the side of the bridge and I got this overwhelming urge to just go full throttle and shut my eyes, straight off the bridge into the Thames, because I didn't want that last little bit of the journey into work. I felt like it would be so much easier to just go over the edge.

But then this happened, so I walked out. The rebel in me felt great. But I was also shaking, thinking I've gone through all of that for nothing.

HAZELNUT-AND-RAISIN-BREAD

Ingredients: makes 2 small or 1 large loaf

35g roast skinned hazelnuts
40g raisins
325g strong white bread flour
185g wholemeal flour
10g salt
15g fresh yeast
300ml water
25g runny honey plus a little
    extra for glazing

To make the bread, set oven to 220°C. Lightly crush the hazelnuts then add to a mixer fitted with the dough hook attachment, along with the raisins and all the other dry ingredients. Start mixing on a slow speed.

Dissolve the yeast in the water with the honey then pour into the dry ingredients. Keep mixing until the dough becomes fairly smooth and elastic. Form into a ball then place in a floured bowl and cover with cling film. Leave at room temperature for about an hour-an-a-half or until doubled in size - you could make the dough the night before and prove to this stage in the fridge overnight.

Once proved, turn out and shape into one or two long loaves depending on preference.

Place onto a floured baking sheet and leave to prove again. This should take about another hour - longer if first proving was done in the fridge - or until doubled in size.

Bake in oven at 220°C for 10 minutes then reduce temperature to 180°C for a further 20 minutes or until bread sounds hollow when tapped on the bottom.

Brush with honey to glaze and leave to cool on a wire rack.

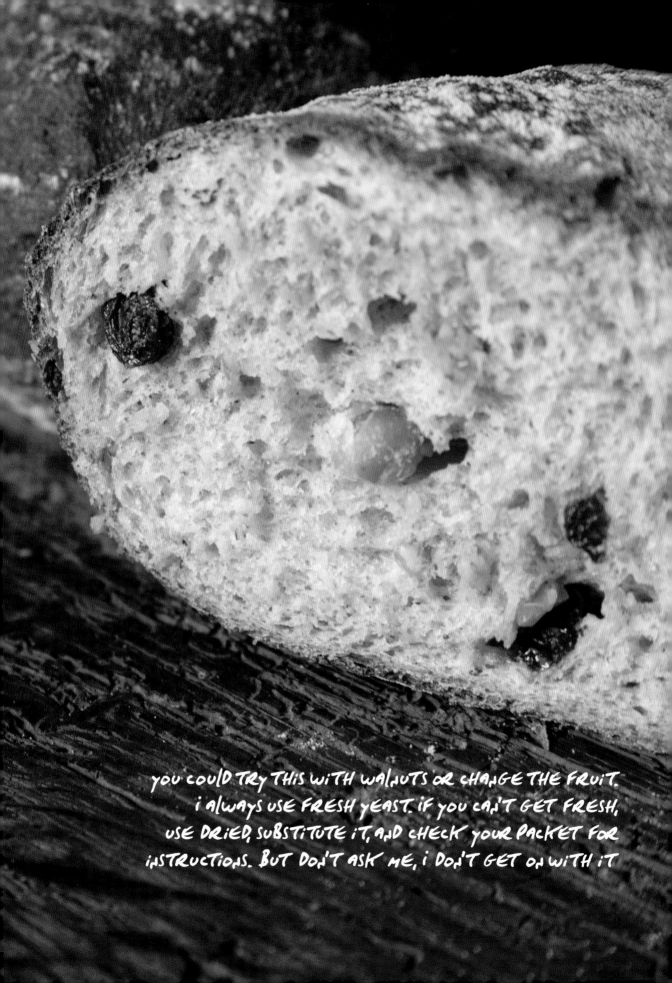

YOU COULD TRY THIS WITH WALNUTS OR CHANGE THE FRUIT.
i ALWAYS USE FRESH YEAST. IF YOU CAN'T GET FRESH,
USE DRIED, SUBSTITUTE IT, AND CHECK YOUR PACKET FOR
INSTRUCTIONS. BUT DON'T ASK ME, i DON'T GET ON WITH IT

FILLET-OF-HAKE, WILD-GARLIC-CROQUETAS, HAM-EMULSION

HAKE ALWAYS MAKES ME THINK OF SPAIN AND IT MAKES SENSE
TO PAIR IT WITH THE BEST SPANISH PRODUCT, THE BEST HAM
IN THE WORLD. THE CROQUETAS ARE A NOD TO THE TAPAS BAR,
AND YOU COULD MAKE THEM WITH HAM, SPINACH, SALT COD, ETC

Ingredients: serves 4

Croquetas
a handful of wild garlic leaves
25g butter
30g flour
250ml milk
salt and white pepper
50g plain flour
2 large free range eggs, beaten
100g panko breadcrumbs

Ham emulsion
250g water
175g Serrano ham
50g Iberico ham fat
90ml Manzanilla sherry
1 shallot, peeled and sliced
4 cloves of garlic, peeled
    and crushed
freshly ground white pepper
a few drops of sherry vinegar

4 fillets of hake, roughly
    150g each
a few hand-carved slices of
    bellotta ham
purple sprouting broccoli

To make the croquetas, heat a little olive oil in a frying pan then sauté the wild garlic leaves until well wilted. Leave to cool before chopping finely.

Melt the butter in a small saucepan then stir in 30g of the flour. Cook for a few minutes then add the cold milk, all in one go.

Bring to the boil, while gently whisking until it starts to thicken. Reduce the heat and continue cooking and stirring for a few minutes. Add the wild garlic and season with fine sea salt and white pepper.

Line a small square plastic container with cling film. Scrape the mix into the container making sure you have a smooth even layer. Chill it in the fridge until cold and set firm.

When set, remove from plastic and cut into cubes, coat in the remaining flour, then egg and then panko. Place on a parchment-lined tray and keep them in the fridge until ready to fry.

To make the ham emulsion, put everything except the vinegar into a pressure cooker. Cook at full pressure for 30 minutes. Leave to cool then strain through a fine sieve, squeezing as much juice as you can out from the ham. Discard all the solids.

To serve, heat a little vegetable oil in a frying pan, season the hake fillets and fry, skin side down until the skin is nice and crisp, and the fish cooked about two-thirds through. Turn and continue to cook for one minute.

Deep fry the croquetas at 180°C until golden. Drain on kitchen paper.

Warm the emulsion and season with the vinegar. Leave to reduce a little if it's too thin.

Blanch a few pieces of sprouting broccoli for about a minute. Put them on the grill to finish cooking and give them a charred flavour, then season with fine sea salt and freshly ground white pepper.

Place the fish on warm plates. Dress with the emulsion and place the croquetas alongside, topped with pieces of Iberico ham and broccoli.

ROSEMARY-FOCACCIA CHELSEA-BUNS

Ingredients: makes 16 buns

Rosemary pesto
3 sprigs fresh rosemary
1 clove garlic, peeled and crushed
5g fine sea salt
20g skinned hazelnuts
150ml extra virgin olive oil

Bread dough
25g fresh yeast
450ml lukewarm water
900g 00 flour
275g of cold mashed potato
10g fine sea salt

To make the pesto, using a food processor, whiz all the rosemary leaves, garlic, salt and hazelnuts to a rough paste. Trickle in the olive oil until all incorporated. It should now look like a pesto. Chill it in the fridge until ready to use.

To make the dough, mix the yeast with approximately 50ml of the water to form a paste.

In the bowl of an electric mixer fitted with a dough hook, mix the flour, potato, yeast and salt. Add the rest of the water and keep mixing or kneading until you have a smooth and springy dough.

Lightly oil another bowl then transfer the dough ball and cover with cling film. Leave at room temperature for about an hour-and-a-half or until the dough has doubled in size.

Using a rolling pin gently roll the dough into a rectangle of about 1cm thick.

Generously spread the pesto all over the dough. You can store any leftover pesto in the fridge and use it to roast potatoes.

Starting with the longest side towards you, roll the dough into a long sausage shape then cut into even pieces of about 3cm.

Oil a deep roasting tray (approximately 36x24cm) and lay each piece of dough flat, side by side so that you can see the spiral.

Set your oven to 220°C. Leave to prove again, this time uncovered for about 30 minutes or until the buns have risen and look a bit puffy.

Drizzle with a little more olive oil. Put in the oven for 10 minutes before reducing the heat to 180°C and baking for another 20 minutes or until golden brown. Remove from the oven and leave to cool in tin for 5 minutes before transferring to a cooling rack. You can now just pull them apart.

They're best served warm but cold's good too.

THIS IS MY IDIOT-PROOF RECIPE. I DEVELOPED IT WHEN
I WAS MOVING TO CHELSEA TO OPEN CHRISTOPH'S. I WANTED A
BREAD FOR THERE. RATHER THAN BAKE IT IN A TRAY,
WE ROLLED IT SO IT LOOKED LIKE A CHELSEA BUN.
A BREAD ROLL FOR THE NEW CHELSEA OPENING

OXTAIL-RISOTTO

I'VE GOT A THING ABOUT RISOTTO, I LOVE IT. THE FIRST
RISOTTOS OF MY LIFE WERE FROM A VESTA PACKET IN
MY CHILDHOOD. ADD BOILING WATER, STIR, REHYDRATE.
IT WAS LIKE MAGIC TO ME, I THOUGHT I WAS COOKING

Ingredients: serves 6

Braised oxtail

1kg oxtail, cut into pieces
    and seasoned
1 large onion, peeled and
    chopped
1 stick of celery, chopped
1 carrot, peeled and sliced
1 tbsp tomato purée
half a bottle of good red wine
350ml brown chicken or beef stock
3 cloves garlic, peeled and crushed
1 large sprig of thyme
2 bay leaves
1 star anise
fine sea salt and ground
    white pepper

Risotto

1 large onion, peeled and
    finely diced
30ml olive oil
a knob of butter
400g carnaroli rice
250ml good red wine
drained stock from the cooked oxtail
fine sea salt
freshly ground black pepper
25g butter
100g freshly grated parmesan

Vegetable garnish

a little olive oil and butter
a knob of butter
50g celeriac, finely diced
50g carrot, finely diced
50g parsnip, finely diced

To make the braised oxtail, in the pan of a pressure cooker, brown the seasoned oxtail pieces in a little vegetable oil then remove. Add all the vegetables and continue to brown. Stir in the tomato purée then add the wine. Let it bubble for a minute then return the oxtail pieces to the pan, along with the stock and all the other ingredients. Pressure cook at full pressure for 45 minutes. Leave to cool.

When cool enough to handle, drain through a sieve. Remove all the meat from the bones and reserve. Remove any fat from the top of the resultant stock and reserve.

To make the risotto, sweat the onion in the oil and knob of butter. Add the rice and stir to coat. Cook the rice for a minute or so before adding the wine and simmer until absorbed. Once the wine has completely disappeared, start adding the hot stock from the braised oxtail a little at a time. Keep stirring and adding stock until all the stock has been absorbed and the rice is just becoming tender. Add the oxtail, season then leave to rest.

To make the vegetable garnish, heat the oil and butter in a frying pan. Add the diced vegetables and continue to roast until soft and golden.

To serve, stir the butter and half the parmesan into the risotto then spoon into the centre of warmed plates. Tap the undersides of the plates to help the risotto spread and find its own level.

Scatter the roast vegetables over the top and sprinkle over the remaining parmesan.

POACHED-OYSTERS, CHORIZO-CREAM, CUCUMBER-GRANITA

Ingredients: serves 4

Cucumber granita
3g fine sea salt
a pinch of sugar
1/2 cucumber, juiced
5ml Chardonnay vinegar

Chorizo cream
250g raw cooking chorizo
1/2 small onion, peeled and
    finely chopped
1/2 carrot, peeled and sliced
1 sprig of thyme
2 cloves of garlic, peeled
    and crushed
125ml dry white wine
300ml white chicken stock
100ml whipping cream

12 rock oysters

To make the cucumber granita, dissolve the salt and sugar in the cucumber juice and vinegar. Freeze it in a shallow container, beating with a fork each time ice crystals start to form.

To make the chorizo cream, remove the skin from the chorizo and cut into smallish pieces. Fry the chorizo in a small saucepan until it starts to release its oil. Add the vegetables, thyme and garlic and continue to sweat them until soft. Add the wine and reduce until almost completely gone. Add the stock and continue to reduce by about two-thirds. Add the cream and simmer for 5 minutes or until it reaches a coating consistency. Pass through a fine sieve.

To serve, shuck the oysters and put them in a small saucepan along with their juices. Wash the bottom shells and place them on a serving plate. Gently warm the oysters until they just start to firm up, this should take no more than 1 minute. Be careful not to overcook them.

Place an oyster in each shell, spoon the chorizo cream over each one and top with the granita.

i USED TO DO A CHORIZO CREAM SOUP AT CHRISTOPH'S, AND PUT AN OYSTER BEIGNET ON TOP IN A LITTLE NEST OF FRESH CUCUMBER 'SPAGHETTI' TO KEEP IT CRISP. THIS IS A VARIATION OF THAT, AS IT USES THE SAME FLAVOURS, BUT WITH A REFRESHING CUCUMBER GRANITA

ORGANIC-SALMON, PASTILLA, BULGAR, PEPPER, BABA-GANOUSH

USE THE BEST FISH YOU CAN, BUT IT DOESN'T HAVE TO BE ORGANIC, ALTHOUGH WILD WOULD BE THE PREFERENCE. IF YOU ARE USING FARMED THEN GLENARM OR VAR ARE DIFFERENT, NOT SO FATTY OR RICH

Ingredients: serves 6

1 side of salmon, approx 1.5kg
a small handful of coriander cress

Pastilla
trim from the salmon, diced
1 tsp lemon zest
30g olive oil
3g ground coriander
3g ground cumin
10g fresh coriander
10g flat leaf parsley leaves
5g mint leaves
3g ras el hanout
3g salt
1 sheet of brik pastry
melted butter

Pepper jam
2 red peppers
a little vegetable oil
1 onion, peeled and finely sliced
5g fine sea salt
10g golden caster sugar
5ml sherry vinegar

Baba ganoush
1 large aubergine
1 clove of garlic, peeled
    and crushed
juice of 1/2 a lemon
5g fine sea salt
10g tahini paste
2g Aleppo pepper flakes

Bulgur salad
150g bulgur wheat
50g barrel-aged feta cheese
2tbsp Greek yoghurt
1/2 cucumber, peeled,
    deseeded and finely diced

Carrot vinaigrette
250ml carrot juice
1 large free range egg yolk
1 tsp Dijon mustard
1 tbsp white miso paste
1 tsp Moscatel vinegar
100ml rapeseed oil
a pinch each of sugar and
    fine sea salt

Prepare the salmon by cutting 6 fillets from the centre of the side, approximately 180–200gms each, save the trim for the pastilla.

To make the pastilla, remove the skin from the remaining salmon and cut the fish into 1cm dice. Blitz all of the remaining pastilla ingredients (except for the pastry and butter) and mix into the diced salmon. Lay the brik pastry on a board and brush it all over with the melted butter. Trim the edges from the pastry to create a square. Put the salmon mixture in a line along the bottom edge and roll it into a sausage. Wrap tightly in cling film and keep it in the fridge.

To make the pepper jam, rub the peppers with oil, and then grill or barbecue until they're charred and blistered. Transfer them to a bowl and cover tightly with cling film. Leave to cool, then peel and deseed them before cutting into thin strips. Sweat the onion and salt for about 30 minutes, or until completely soft. Add the sugar and vinegar and continue to cook until lightly golden. Add the peppers and cook for another 10 minutes, or until sticky and jam-like.

To make the baba ganoush, prick the aubergine all over with a fork. Grill (preferably on a barbecue to achieve an authentic smoky flavour) until soft and completely collapsed. Once cool enough to handle, scrape the flesh from the inside, discarding the skin. Drain off any excess liquid before mashing to a rough pulp, with the rest of the ingredients.

To make the bulgur salad, put the bulgur wheat into a bowl and pour on enough boiling water to just cover. Immediately cover the bowl tightly with cling film. Leave to stand for 15 minutes, before fluffing up with a fork. In a separate bowl, mash the feta and yoghurt together to form a rough purée. Fold this through the wheat along with the cucumber.

To make the carrot vinaigrette, concentrate the carrot juice by boiling until reduced by two-thirds. Put the yolk, mustard, miso and vinegar into a bowl or blender. Add the carrot juice, then gradually whisk in the oil. Check the seasoning before adding salt and sugar.

To serve, fry the salmon fillets in a little vegetable oil, skin side down, until crisp and cooked two-thirds of the way through. Turn and cook for a further minute. Cut the pastilla into 6 equal pieces. Remove the cling film then in a separate pan, colour them evenly in a little oil until crisp and golden.

Place a spoon of pepper, aubergine and bulgur on each plate, along with a salmon fillet and pastilla. Drizzle with the carrot vinaigrette and garnish with coriander cress.

I'D BEEN TALKING TO
RICHARD CORRIGAN ABOUT
WORKING TOGETHER

THE-HOUSE

"I liked him, and it was real. It was about food. I felt like I would get back to cooking."

Richard came up with a deal, a partnership, and we shook hands in his front room. Although I still didn't know what we were going to be doing together, because he was keeping a lot of things in the air. In the end I went to give his sous chef Malcolm a hand as he was just opening a new place. Corrigan had been trying to keep me away from Malcolm, because Malcolm was a nut case. Anyway, I met this famous nut job, Malcolm, who was manic, and mental. We got on like a house on fire. We ended up like brothers through my whole time with Corrigan. We're still really good mates. Without Malcolm, I couldn't have opened The West House.

He is mad, but he's also one of the best cooks I've ever met.

I helped Malcolm for a matter of weeks at The English Garden, not long at all, because part of the deal when they bought that was that they had to take The English House around the corner. And they didn't know what to do with it. So they said I could do what I wanted, run it as my own place. The English House was falling down, they only wanted The English Garden, so they put all their money into that. I wanted my own restaurant at this point and I didn't want to go and work for anybody else again. But with Corrigan I was being given an opportunity to run my own restaurant. It was my last go at doing it with someone else's money.

The agreement was I'd take it on as chef patron, run it on my own as a partner.

In the meantime I was helping Malcolm. Then Corrigan rang me up after a couple of weeks and said, "You've got to go around to The House now, it's just bleeding money. It's killing me." It was still running as it had been with the chef they inherited. So I went to have a look, to walk around. I'd already eaten there, before I agreed to it all. It was atrocious.

I took Jackie with me, and we sat and had lunch and didn't let on who we were. We left half the food.

This time I walked in the kitchen, I think it was a Friday lunchtime, during my break. The restaurant door was locked, I rang the bell and got no answer. The kitchen hatch was open, so I walked down the hatch, had a look, had a little mosey about, as there was no one in the kitchen. It was all very clean. I phoned Richard, told him I was round there, and that there was no one there but it was very clean. He did his nut! Of course it's clean, it's so clean because they're not doing any fucking covers!

So they arranged for me to go in there, meet the chef and start. I phoned Barry, and told him we'd start Monday. We planned to go in, just the two of us, and work with the chef. I'd written a menu, but thought we'd go in, let them do their service and observe. So we got in there, I met him and his sous chef, and we let them get on with lunch. It was absolutely appalling! Microwave pies in a dish with puff pastry on top, loads of shit bread in the freezer, and he'd made gallons of sauce to get us started. Baz tasted it and with his famous lack of tact, started chucking it all in the bin! It wasn't endearing us to the chef. I thought we should clean the fridges out and run through the menu, start prepping and gradually change it all by the Friday. Oh, they didn't like that at all! They did the lunch service and then both disappeared. I went up to the office looking for them and I just caught them coming down with their coats on. Both of them walked out and left me and Baz standing there.

Somehow we got it together. I changed the restaurant from The English House to The House, got a sign written, and ran it as my own place. I didn't go as far as putting my name over the door because I didn't really think that was the right thing to do.

decor may be
dgy, but lovers of
glish food will feel
nome at The House

We did the menus, set the restaurant up, and Corrigan came in and absolutely loved what we were doing. It all started to build, and within weeks AA Gill came in and gave us the best review ever. The story goes that at Christoph's he had given me a good review, of which the main course made it to The London Magazine's dishes of the week. But when it became Nico Chelsea, Gill came in and absolutely destroyed us. He criticised the location of the restaurant. He criticised the door, he criticised the colour of the door, he criticised everything there was and then was vicious about the food and the service and everything else. I couldn't understand; I didn't see how he could criticise the location or the door when it was the same restaurant as Christoph's! Then I got summoned to Nico who told me to ignore it, that it was purely personal, a thing between the two of them. I was told it had nothing to do with me, not to let it bother me. But it does, I was the chef. I felt a real twat. You get over it but it was awful, devastating, it was the worst review I've ever had of anything.

And then there he was at The House. I went upstairs and looked round, and the first thing I saw was 'the blonde', AA Gill's missus. I went straight downstairs in a blind panic and phoned Richard. He said to make a point of saying hello to him, that it's always harder to criticise someone if they can put a face to you. I thought that was good advice. So when he'd been fed I went up and was sort of hovering behind this pillar behind them. But I didn't know what to do because I don't know him. He got up to walk out and as he stood up, I walked round the corner, put my hand on his shoulder and said, "Adrian do us a favour, don't put me out of another fucking job, eh! You destroyed me at Nico's, don't do it again here."

When the paper came out his column described this scenario in which a crazed, unshaven, sleep-deprived chef, was hovering, loitering to accost him.

He wrote about what I had said. And that it prompted a conversation between him and his missus on the way home, in which he was very flippant and she had a go at him about his effect on people's lives and jobs. He had ended up sleeping on the couch. He then gave me the best review that he'd ever given anybody, about every single dish. He ended the review by writing, "So, there you go, Graham [he never name-checks chefs], there's the good review that you wanted, but for a good meal, and a great restaurant."

It became a big deal wherever I went for the best part of a year. I became quite well known as the man that made AA Gill sleep on the couch. That was pivotal in us doing really well, in this shit-hole that hadn't even been refurbed.

One day a regular customer, Sir Geoffrey Shakerley, phoned me up saying that a very good friend of his, Lady Westmorland, was having a dinner party. He had suggested one of our private rooms, but she was very nervous about it. Would it be all right if he popped in with her? He arranged to come by, and we went upstairs to a private dining room, sat down and talked through menus. She wanted to bring about ten people, and was very nervous because one of the guests was quite tricky, she had to know it would be suitable for her. Sir Geoffrey was explaining that it would be fine, that she could leave it with me, I would sort everything out and she didn't have to worry. She said that it was a very important guest, who didn't go out much. That she wanted to bring the Queen! I said we got a lot of people here and that she could trust us. I was trying to reassure her it'd be fine, and dismissed it, batty old cow!

So, off she went and I told everyone that apparently she wanted to bring her mate the Queen! They laughed and we did a menu for her private party.

"Her Majesty The Queen had her shoes off under the table, it was great."

Her Majesty the Queen had been in Italy and there been a big deal in the paper about her not liking garlic. That stuck because it was big news. Slow news day. I just remember thinking that no one had said anything to me about dietary requirements or her not liking garlic, so I wrote a menu accordingly, laced with garlic.

On the day, we'd done lunch, cleared down and were just about to try and get out for a coffee. Suddenly two guys came down the stairs in long coats with ear-pieces. One came up and put his hand on my shoulder, called me Graham and introduced himself. He knew who I was. At this point Barry and our other chef both shot out the hatch and did a runner. They thought the police were there, so they legged it.

He said he was the Head of Security for Buckingham Palace, and the Queen's personal detective. The other bloke was the Head of New Scotland Yard. They wanted me to show them the rooms where the party would eat and have drinks, and all access to them. Because Lady Westmorland was bringing Her Majesty and the Defence Minister to dinner! They scoped everything out, checking the roof to see where they would put snipers, which doors they would have to guard or keep locked. Then they checked the restaurant bookings, asked if we had a free table for a plain-clothes couple. And he went through the book checking who they knew and who they needed to run a check on.

They all arrived at eight, though I didn't see as I was in the kitchen. I did a starter with baked brioche, in a savarin mould, with mushrooms and a poached egg in the hole. It was basically mushrooms on toast. Their main course was sea bass with saffron risotto. I gave them a cheese course, a vacherin with bread at either end of the table, so that they had to pass it around and get stuck in.

It got to about quarter to midnight, I was standing on the stairs and you could hear all the laughter upstairs. I asked the security guy if that was normal. He said it wasn't, that they were obviously having a good time. I asked if she did a lot of that kind of thing. He answered no, they didn't, that it was all engagements, official dinners and stuff. She hadn't been out to a private dinner party with a friend in something like 12 years.

When they came walking down the stairs I was standing at the bottom, in my dirty apron. Sir Geoffrey introduced me as Graham, the chef, and she stopped, turned round, and shook my hand. We stood and had a chat for quite a little while. I don't know what the protocol should have been, she was just like any nice customer. It's weird though, she had a bit of an aura about her. She was a really polite, nice old lady, who was just very gracious and thanked me for the meal, saying how wonderful it was.

At The House I used to do pork belly and scallops. So it was on the menu one lunchtime when a French waiter came to me and said there were two guys upstairs, one of whom was American and wanted to talk to me about the food. The American wants to talk to me about the pork belly. I was knackered, I couldn't be bothered to hear him tell me that back in America the pigs are much bigger. I told him to fuck off. But apparently they were in a private room, waiting until I'd finished. I asked the waiter to tell them I'd gone. At which point I went upstairs to the phone. All of a sudden a guy came up, an English guy, and said it was great to meet me. I thought I recognised him and then he introduced himself as Tom Stoppard. He said he was a big fan, and ate with us lots. He started telling me about some of the dishes he'd had.

"He said he was there with someone who was really raving about the pork. And he wanted to know, if I didn't mind, how I cooked it, because he was a really keen cook. Apparently it was the best pork belly he'd ever had. Of course I said fine, okay. So this guy came up to meet me, walked in and it was fucking Harrison Ford! He came in and said "Hi, I'm Harrison." And I was thinking "It's fucking Han Solo!" It turned out he cooks a fair bit and was really interested in it all."

INDIANA JONES LIKED
MY PORK BELLY

TREACLE-SODA-BREAD

Ingredients: makes 1 loaf

125g wholemeal flour
60g self-raising flour
60g pinhead oatmeal
30g bran
15g wheatgerm
5g sea salt
5g bicarbonate of soda
30g black treacle
300ml buttermilk,
        see page 26

To make the soda bread, set your oven to 175°C. Place all dry ingredients in a bowl. Dissolve black treacle into the buttermilk then stir into the dry ingredients creating a big sticky mess.

Scrape the contents of the bowl onto a well-floured surface and shape the dough into a ball. Transfer to a floured baking tray. Using a very sharp knife, make a cross on the top.

Bake for around 45 minutes at 175°C, until your bread sounds hollow when tapped on its bottom. Leave to cool on a wire rack for as long as you can resist.

THIS IS BASED ON A RECIPE GIVEN TO ME BY MALCOLM STARMER, WHEN WORKING AT THE HOUSE. IT'S GREAT TO SERVE WITH CHEESE, CREAM CHEESE AND SMOKED SALMON, PICKLED OR CURED FISH AND HORSERADISH, AND IT'S BEST WHEN IT'S FRESH. IT'S ALSO GREAT TOASTED WITH SCRAMBLED EGGS

CURED-FOIE-GRAS, DUCK CONFIT, PICKLED-RHUBARB, GINGERBREAD

Ingredients: serves 24

This is very much a restaurant dish that I had to include by popular demand. You can scale it down to serve less people, but this is how it's done at The West House.

Cured foie gras
1 lobe of foie gras
30g Banyuls
30g Monbazillac
5g fine sea salt
1/2 tsp pink salt
a pinch of sugar
a few grinds of black pepper
enough coarse sea salt to cover

Confit cure
150g coarse sea salt
20 crushed black peppercorns
1 head of garlic, peeled
2 star anise
1/2 bunch of thyme
2 bay leaves

Duck confit
6 large fatty duck legs
2 banana shallots, peeled and finely diced
1 large sprig of thyme
100ml Armagnac

Parfait reduction
100g Madeira
100g ruby port
50g brandy
2 banana shallots, peeled and sliced
3 cloves of garlic, peeled and crushed
1 large sprig of thyme
1 bay leaf

Parfait
200g foie gras (from the lobe)
200g chicken livers
4 large free range eggs
400g butter, melted
freshly ground white pepper
10g fine sea salt

Rhubarb chutney
1kg rhubarb
150g golden caster sugar
120g water
120g liquid glucose
150g white wine vinegar
2tbsp hibiscus flowers

Gingerbread
170g butter
120g black treacle
120g golden syrup
200g dark soft brown sugar
450g plain flour
10g mixed spice
10g ground ginger
15g baking powder
5g bicarbonate of soda
5g fine sea salt
2 large free range eggs
550ml milk

To cure the foie gras, soften the foie gras lobe at room temperature then remove all the veins. Cut 200gm off and save for the parfait. Sprinkle the rest of the ingredients (except the coarse salt) over the remaining foie gras and place in a vacuum pack bag, or plastic container, and leave in the fridge overnight.

Remove from the fridge and bring to room temperature to soften, and then roll tightly in muslin. Bury in coarse salt, making sure it's completely covered. Refrigerate it for 24 hours.

Unwrap and discard the muslin. Wrap it in cling film and then freeze it.

To make the duck confit, blitz together all of the cure ingredients, then rub all over the duck legs. Put them in a covered container and refrigerate for 24 hours.

Wash the legs in cold water to remove all the salt. Vacuum pack and cook in a water bath at 88°C for 6 hours.

If you don't have a water bath, put the legs in a pan or deep tray, cover with some duck fat and cook in a very low oven for about 2 hours, or until very tender.

When cool enough to handle, remove from the fat, then pick all the meat into a bowl. Discard the bones. (You can keep the skin for another dish).

Sweat the shallots and picked thyme in a little of the rendered duck fat. Add them to the duck meat along with the Armagnac. Check the seasoning, then using cling film, roll into a neat ballotine. Store in the fridge.

To make the parfait, put the reduction ingredients into a non-reactive pan and reduce until almost dry. Scrape the reduction into a blender (removing the bay and thyme sprig) along with the rest of the parfait ingredients. Blitz until smooth. Put the mix into a vacuum pack bag. Seal and cook for 30 minutes at 63°C. Pour into a blender and blitz again then decant into a bowl and refrigerate to set.

To cook the parfait conventionally, blitz and pass the mix through a fine sieve into an oven-proof container. Cover with a disc of parchment and a piece of foil. Cook in the oven in a bain-marie at 130°C for about 40 minutes to 1 hour. Leave it to cool, and then refrigerate.

To make the rhubarb chutney, place everything in a non-reactive pan. Cover and bring to a boil. Remove the lid and continue to cook, stirring occasionally, until thick. Put in a blender and blitz to a smooth, glossy purée.

To make the gingerbread, melt the butter, treacle, syrup and sugar in a pan, being careful not to burn. Mix the flour, mixed spice, ginger, baking powder, bicarbonate of soda and salt. Beat in the eggs then the milk to make a smooth batter. Add the melted sugar mixture.

Pour into a lined and greased cake or loaf tin and bake at 180°C for about 45 minutes. Leave to cool on a rack. When cool, slice thinly and dry in a very low oven until crisp.

To serve, put a slice of duck ballotine in a bowl, and pipe a little rhubarb chutney next to it. Top with a quenelle of parfait and a gingerbread crisp. Grate the frozen cured foie gras all over.

CURED-FOIE-GRAS,DUCK
CONFIT,PICKLED-RHUBARB,
GINGERBREAD

THIS HAS BECOME A BIT OF A SIGNATURE DISH AT THE WEST HOUSE. I HAVE SOME CUSTOMERS WHO EAT IT ALMOST WEEKLY, AND WOULD REVOLT IF I DIDN'T KEEP IT ON THE MENU AND INCLUDE IT HERE

GRAPPA-MARINATED PEACHES, LEMON-VERBENA, MASCARPONE

Ingredients: serves 6

Lemon verbena granita
50g lemon verbena leaves
pinch of salt
50g golden caster sugar
225ml water

Marinated peaches
6 ripe peaches
45g golden caster sugar
45ml grappa

200g mascarpone
1 punnet of raspberries

To make the granita, blanch the verbena in salted boiling water for 5 seconds, refresh in iced water. Drain and dry the leaves. Put them in the blender with the sugar and 225ml of water, then blitz till smooth. Freeze in a shallow container, beating with a fork each time ice crystals start to form.

To marinate the peaches, stone the fruit and cut 4 of them into wedges and the remaining 2 into thin slices. Lay them on a tray and sprinkle all over with the sugar and the grappa. Leave to marinate at room temperature for 1 hour.

To serve, arrange the peaches on your plates along with a few raspberries. Put a dollop of mascarpone in the middle of each plate and spoon the granita all over.

IF YOU CAN GET GREAT WHITE-FLESHED PEACHES IN THEIR PRIME
THEN DO, IF NOT USE YELLOW. THE QUALITY IS MORE IMPORTANT
THAN THE COLOUR. IT'S ALL VERY SIMPLE, PEACHES AND CREAM,
AND THE COMBINATION OF PEACHES AND RASPBERRIES IS CLASSIC

OATCAKES

Ingredients: makes 8-12 biscuits

150g wholemeal flour
140g pinhead oatmeal
5g fine sea salt
15g golden caster sugar
15g celery salt
225g cold butter, diced
85g egg white

To make the oatcakes, put all the dry ingredients in a food processor and whiz to mix everything together. Add the butter and pulse to form a crumb. With the machine running, add the egg white until it all comes together into a sticky dough. Wrap in cling film and put it in the fridge to rest for about half an hour or until you need it.

Remove from fridge and leave until just soft enough to roll.

Line a board with baking parchment, roll the dough onto the parchment to a thickness of about 5mm then place it in the fridge to firm up. Cut into neat rectangles or any shape you fancy. Arrange on a baking tray and bake at 180°C for 12 minutes. Cool the biscuits on a wire rack then store in an airtight container.

THIS WOULD WORK AS A BASE FOR A TART. OURS HAVE A
LOT OF SALT AND CELERY SALT, BUT YOU COULD PLAY THAT
DOWN, DEPENDING ON WHAT YOU ARE USING THEM FOR

WE CALL THIS AN IRISH COFFEE AS IT'S LAYERED, SO YOU DRINK
THE HOT SOUP THROUGH THE COLD CREAM. YOU DON'T USE
A SPOON, JUST PICK IT UP AND DRINK. WE SERVE IT WITH
DOUGHNUTS, AS A PLAY ON COFFEE AND DOUGHNUTS

Ingredients: serves 6

Soup
1 small butternut squash
50g butter
1 sprig of thyme
5g fine sea salt
750ml light chicken or
    vegetable stock
freshly ground white pepper

Doughnuts
85ml milk
10g fresh yeast
45g golden caster sugar
300g plain flour
pinch of salt
1 large free range eggs,
    lightly beaten
30g butter, melted
dried cep powder
grated parmesan

Parmesan cream
100ml whipping cream
50g grated parmesan
250ml milk

To make the soup, peel and remove the seeds from the squash. Slice very thinly. Melt the butter in a saucepan, and add the squash, thyme and salt then cook gently until completely soft. In a separate pan, bring the stock to the boil and then pour over the squash. Continue to simmer for 5 minutes, transfer to a blender, add a few grinds of pepper then blitz until silky smooth.

To make the doughnuts, warm the milk a little. Dissolve the yeast in the milk, with a teaspoon of the sugar.

Put the flour, remaining sugar and salt into the bowl of your mixer. Add the yeast mixture, followed by the egg and the melted butter.

Carry on mixing at a medium speed for about 10 minutes or until the dough is smooth and coming away from the sides of the bowl. Form the dough into a ball and place in a greased bowl. Cover the bowl with cling film and refrigerate it overnight.

On a floured board, roll out the dough to just under 1cm thick. Cover with cling film and put it back in the fridge to chill and firm up a bit.

Using a small round pastry cutter carefully cut out the doughnuts and lay them on greased sheet. Leave them in a warmish place to prove for about 30 minutes.

Set your fryer to 190°C. Carefully fry the doughnuts in batches, a few at a time for a minute or two on each side. Drain on some kitchen paper, before tossing in cep powder and parmesan.

To make the parmesan cream, heat the cream in a small saucepan, remove from the heat then using a hand blender, blend in the cheese. Pour into a cream whipper gun along with the milk and charge with one gas canister.

To serve, pour the hot soup into glasses. Squirt the parmesan cream on top. Serve the doughnuts on the side.

ON-A-WING AND-A-PRAYER

THE HOUSE WAS DOING SO WELL

We couldn't get any more people in, so apparently there was no point in refurbishing or spending any money on it, it would be a waste. But there were mushrooms growing on the toilet wall, I kid you not, like the big things you get on the bark of trees. The décor was that of an old English house, with padded fabric walls, it was really bizarre. There was an asbestos ceiling in the kitchen that used to crumble down, and several health and safety issues. I had to change things.

But they weren't spending any money, the lease was coming to an end, and our partnership deal had never materialised. In the end they decided the best thing would be for me to buy the restaurant off them, and were going to come up with a deal. We were looking at different ways to make it work, but it wasn't making that much sense to me. I didn't want to be travelling to Chelsea and it was too expensive for the family to live there. There was so much money needed to make it right, and since I had made it a success it was an expensive business to buy!

I really wanted a pub, so I started looking. I loved and lost one in Newbury, and was devastated by that. The agent asked me why I was looking out that way, said that the M3/M4 corridor had been done to death. He suggested I come down to Kent, which was totally unknown to me. I'd been to Canterbury, Margate and to Leeds Castle, but I didn't know they were in Kent. The only thing I knew was in Kent was Sevenoaks, because during the great hurricane of '87 they lost some oak trees. It was a big news story that there were no longer seven oaks in Sevenoaks. And I knew that it was called the Garden of England. I knew about the produce.

I knew about apples, I knew about the The National Fruit Collection in Brogdale, I knew about Kentish strawberries and asparagus. You've got the coast, and it's kind of Britain's larder.

So once I found out those other places were in Kent and that East Sussex was close (my brother lived in East Sussex), it seemed a perfect location. The agent put together a little programme of places to look at. I came down and he took me to a couple of pubs, none of which really did it for me. Then he said that before we headed back, he just had to pop in to pick up paperwork from some people that were closing down, and he took me into The West House.

A devious fucker he was. Anyway, I went in and I got that little feeling when you walk in somewhere and think, I like this, this could work. It was a restaurant and I didn't want a restaurant, I wanted a pub. But I had a little look and when I went away it stayed in the back of my mind. So I drove down one Sunday with Jackie. We went to a local restaurant and it was rammed on a Sunday, so quite clearly there was a market there.

I had a good scout around, I looked at all the restaurants and I couldn't find anyone selling anything from Kent. There was no Kentish asparagus, there was no game, there was nothing like that. I went into places and was given shitty frozen fish and it didn't make sense. Where were the scallops from Rye? Kent has so much going on. I came up with this plan to come down here and source everything from within a 10-mile radius. I was going to be completely Kentish, self-sufficient. And be more of a bistro, a local restaurant that you could pop out to because you don't want to cook that night, or somewhere you could have a family celebration, all things to everybody.

That ideal doesn't work for various reasons, you can't be all things to all people. But I still wanted to be the local restaurant, so I didn't write anything in cheffy terms, there were very basic descriptions on the menu, and the food was pretty simple.

I was on my own so it had to be. It was all about the produce and I thought it was good value: £24.50 for three courses, which included all the breads and the usual bits. But I still got flak for it. I remember that first Saturday, just popping up the shop to get a paper and as I got to our door I could hear people looking at the menu board outside. I stopped and listened and I heard this woman say, "Who the hell does he think he is coming down here with his fancy London prices?" to which I yanked the door open and said, "You don't have to fucking come in, do you?" Not the best way to start off!

I didn't have any support in Kent, I didn't know anybody that supplies anything. It helped that it's only an hour on the train from London. It had a little school opposite, the lollipop man stood in our doorway. Jake was 10 and Jess was eight. So it was no effort to take them to school, the lollipop man just took them, across the road. It was a bit like going back to the 70s, unlike how it had become in London. The village seemed quite idyllic and I had the little village restaurant. I thought I could make it work, and if I couldn't then we were buggered. My exit strategy to this day is called a wooden box, that's my way out.

We'd got the restaurant, we'd live upstairs and as long as I could make enough to pay the bank back I'd got a roof over my head. I remember once staring at the big inglenook fireplace that's in the restaurant thinking, I wonder if I could put some kind of pizza oven in there and turn it into a pizza takeaway, whatever, if that's what it takes to pay the bills.

So, that was it really. I was on my own in the kitchen. I won't lie, it was bloody stressful, and very tense. There was screaming and shouting because I'm not the easiest person. I was under a lot of pressure and I was also a screamy shouty London chef. And then suddenly I was on my own.

Jackie hadn't done any waitressing or any of that kind of work. She'd worked in the dealing room of a big American bank, and then after the kids she was working on a foreign currency counter. I said to just try and learn the admin side and help with that, which she was quite keen to take on, to get involved and support in that way. Then of course the reality was we had to get open and if she could just serve a couple of people? She was terrified, but she sort of agreed, and our deal was that we'd strip it back. I had a list, one of those magazine lists, of the most annoying things for customers in restaurants; being faffed over, having people constantly topping up your wine, upselling water, and I decided not to do any of that, because anyway I hate it. We wanted a relaxed restaurant, with no tablecloths, which is very trendy now but wasn't then. It had to be more about the food. Plus the less I had to spend on staffing and faffing around, the more I could spend on the food. And maybe we could charge less. That philosophy wasn't 100% my own, I took a lot from what Shaun Hill had done at The Merchant House out in Ludlow.

So, Jackie had to help. I always remember opening night because I had a list, a service plan from Nico. Bear in mind this was from his three-star place, so it starts with coming in, polishing all the glasses, polishing all the bottles, setting up a restaurant. It had everything right through the whole of service, including the meet and greet. I gave that to Jackie, and said there's your plan, that's what you do, that's how you do it. I added my tuppence-worth on top of that. The most important thing was to always greet people with a smile, don't leave them hanging, and the same when they leave. Never let them leave, no matter what you are doing, without a 'thank you for coming to our restaurant'. And the rest we'll muddle through. Any questions from customers, just come and ask me.

"I told her it would only be to get us up and running. Thirteen years on and she's still there. I lied!"

Jake was in the kitchen and that caused the biggest problems. He was 10 and like most 10-year-olds, he was all excited. He used to come to Chelsea with me sometimes on the back of my bike, which Jackie didn't like much, but he used to like coming to work and having a bit of laugh. In London I wasn't seeing the kids at all, I was missing the football matches, the school plays, everything. In The West House I could see them go down the stairs in the morning to the lollipop man and they'd come home at night, I'd make them something to eat. I'd see them on a daily basis. I might still be in the kitchen and working but I'd see them.

Jake was there, all keen, and after a while he was making bread, he was making biscuits, then he was crying because his hands were cold where he had to scrub five kilo of mussels, and he hated picking spinach. And I was just telling him to do it and stop fucking moaning. "I wanna do something more interesting, it's boring!" Well that's what cooking is, a series of boring repetitive tasks, live with it. In the end, in an effort to appease him, I got him to bone out and butcher the chickens. Jackie was moaning because he'd butchered chickens with a knife at 10 years old. I didn't see the problem, as he was doing it fine. But she was really bothered at me shouting at him. I was really on his case the whole time. It put him off the kitchen, which wasn't a bad thing. He only came back into it because he was caught buying beer from a local offy for some friends, who asked him to go in and get it because he was tall. A plain-clothes police officer was watching the place because they were selling to under-age kids. So as part of Jake's punishment, I put him in the kitchen on the pot wash. It was only supposed to be until I deemed fit that he'd paid his dues. But he's worked with us ever since, he must have been about 14.

He progressed from washing up into using the coffee machine, and then helping Jackie a bit. He gravitated towards the front of house, staying away from the kitchen side.

Jake was also very into music, so when he was a bit older I got him work experience via Tony Taverner, our record producer, who was running a company called In Flight where they do all the music programmes for airlines. He got on really great with those guys and was angling for a job when he came to leave school. But when he came to it he didn't want to give up restaurants, so he made a decision to stay. I said that if he was going to do it, treat it as a career and do it properly, which he has done.

We opened on the 21st June, Midsummer's Day. I survived on friends coming down and helping, Malcolm especially. Phil Jones, the crazy Welshman who bears an uncanny resemblance to Chris Evans and was one of my right-hand men in the Nico days, used to come too. They would turn up on a Friday afternoon, sometimes if they weren't working it'd be a Thursday night to be there for the Friday prep, but other than that they'd come down Friday afternoon and do Friday service, then Saturday night and go home Sunday afternoon. June 2002 wasn't particularly busy, I remember counting the money on my very first weekend thinking, "I've taken enough to pay the bank."

Michelin came and inspected us for the very first time in March of the next year. I think it was Rebecca Burr before she was the boss, she was the first one in to my knowledge.

That summer we had a write-up in Waitrose magazine. We were building local business by word of mouth.

Then it got towards the end of the year and I got a note from Jennifer Sharp who was then editor of Harper's & Queen, she'd been down as well. She came for lunch on a Sunday and loved it, she thought the whole thing was really cool. Then I got a card from her and an invite to the Moët & Chandon Harper's & Queen Restaurant Awards at Claridges. There was a note scribbled on it saying, 'It's on a Monday, I know it's your day off so you've got no excuse not to come. Jennifer'.

The day of the event we had the extraction being cleaned. The restaurant was busy, so Monday was the only day to do our accounts. We had the accountant down, and it was a nightmare day, it was the only day I could do anything other than cook. I used to prep Friday night for Saturday, make desserts at 2 o'clock in the morning after Saturday night and clear down on my own. I don't know how I did it! Anyway it got to the afternoon and although we ummed and aaahed, Mum and Dad were there to look after the kids and I thought we should go. We walked into this main hall, and everyone was there. Raymond Blanc was standing with his arm on my shoulder and a few people came around to say hi. Angus Deayton was the host and then they came to the category for the Best Restaurant Outside of London. The nominees were...
The Vineyard at Stock Cross... Le Manoir Aux Quat'Saisons... The West House in Biddenden.... I fucking dropped my glass! I'd had no idea. Everybody was patting me on the back and although we didn't win it didn't matter.

> "The Michelin Guide always came out in January then. I remember being at the sink, I was picking curly kale into the running water and the radio was on."

The news came on and it said that the Fat Duck had just gained its third Michelin star. I was thinking about Richard and Malcolm in London, wondering who'd got what. The press release was out, and sometimes they have stuff like that in The Times, so I told Jackie to go up the shop, grab a paper and see if there was anything in it. So she ran off and as she did the phone rang. I picked the phone up and it was Charles Campion saying, "I hear congratulations are in order, old boy", and I said, "Really, for what?" "You haven't heard? Let me be the first to tell you, you've got a star."

I was kind of hoping, if I got anything, my ambition would have been to get a Bib Gourmand, because I never thought I was worthy of a star. I started cooking too late, I wasn't part of that set. Stars were just beyond the realms. If I had started younger and not done the music, then maybe.

When he said I had a star I was a bit shocked. I thought it was a wind-up, that it couldn't actually be Charles. "Okay," he said. "You obviously need to see this in print. Stand by your fax machine." So I stood there and watched it come through, and at the very top, because the new ones come first and it's done alphabetically, it said, Biddenden The West House, One Star.

So we got the star pretty quickly, about 18 months after opening. Attention started to build. Nick Lander came and reviewed us. He and Jancis Robinson know Richard Corrigan and they were chatting about me. In the end, most of the national papers came our way. Which without a PR company is not bad.

And there has been some TV. I got a phone call from a TV production company saying they were making this programme featuring restaurants, and that turned out to be Taste of the South. It was on ITV and the whole episode was pretty much us.

The people from Great British Menu came down and did a screen test with me for the second series. I couldn't commit to the amount of time that I potentially needed to be available to film. I was on my own in the kitchen then. It would have shut us down, and we couldn't afford that, financially or professionally. So I couldn't do it.

Then I got asked to make a show called Food Poker for the BBC. There were to be chefs sitting round a table, who would be dealt cards, but instead of playing cards, they would be food ingredients cards. You would be dealt a hand of ingredients cards and have to create a dish out of the hand that you are dealt. You would pitch your dish to a live studio audience and they would choose the two dishes they wanted to see, which led to a live cook-off battle. That was quite good fun, I did well on it. And if you didn't cook you got to taste and comment. But they didn't commission it for a second series.

In 2010 TV called again, about another show, saying we'd been voted as one of the best restaurants in the UK. I hadn't seen anything out there, any competitions or anything. But they said I'd been voted for by my customers. So I agreed in principle to this TV show about Britain's best restaurants. Then there were all these interviews and they came down. They were really cagey about the whole project. We ended up in the finals of the English restaurant category. It wasn't until a bit later that we were told Gordon Ramsay was involved, until then we had no idea that it was anything to do with him.

Once they had done lots of filming of us at The West House, they said that the next thing was a series of challenges. What?! I was in a game show, a reality fucking game show. So next we had to do the Mystery Diner sequence. And then have a coach-load of 30 people descend on us.

We were a little bit angsty to say the least. It was a tough one, but we agreed we had to go the distance, see it through. And I was proud to make it to the final and of what me and Ben cooked.

The reaction was mental, when it came on TV. Ramsay was screaming and shouting and I was staring at him and making it look very provocative. The phone just started ringing off the hook downstairs. By halfway through that programme, we couldn't take any internet bookings because we'd brought down the servers. And our telephone was just ridiculous and the answerphone actually broke, cheap as fuck. Suddenly we had 50 people booked for the day, every day. I limited our covers to 20 for lunch, which is a lot for us, and 30 for dinner. That was it. Every day for six months, with two of us.

I finally did do Great British Menu in their seventh season, which was in 2012. By then we had been open 10 years, with the Michelin star since early days, and it felt a little bit more possible to leave and spend time on it at that point. I was representing London and the South East. Jason Atherton was our judge. Phil Howard was competing with me, and so was Marcus McGuinness. All three of us were new to the show, which had never happened in a heat before. I remember when I turned up to cook in the studio Phil Howard was in there leaning against the sink, on his own. He had a big smile and he came and shook hands straight away. He said he was really pleased he was with me, that our food had a lot in common, nothing weird and experimental for the sake of it, all about the food. I was standing there listening in a daze thinking, it's Phil Howard, I've been googled by Phil Howard.

Of course there are a lot of similarities, I steal shitloads from him. I found it really weird. He was very nervous of the whole thing, he'd never done anything like that before. He said it was the first time he'd put his head above the parapet.

Great British Menu was hard, I felt drained when I'd finished, but also that sense of euphoria that I'd achieved something. Phil Howard called the next day, just after the regional final. I didn't know the results yet. He said they had missed me, that it hadn't been the same without me. I asked how he got on and he said he won. That was great, that was one for real cooking. It was a good week. It was the London and South East week, which is the strongest and toughest. I was up against two two-star chefs, Marcus was head chef of two-Michelin-starred Hibiscus. It was a good thing to do, a good time and an achievement.

Phil's a god, and it was cool, there was solidarity between the three of us. The atmosphere was great and it was a really pleasurable thing. Of course you want to win, but after I went out I got texts and calls, from Tom Kerridge, David Everitt-Matthias, people I was chuffed to hear from, saying that I'd smashed it.

When I first started cooking I was in denial about my past, not going to concerts, not listening to music much, immersing myself in food. I have felt awkward about it. The best illustration being that during my first chance at a TV break they wanted me to play pots and pans with wooden spoons. That really sums it up! I think that's why I've always felt a little bit awkward about the whole thing. It's only when I got more comfortable and confident that I started to open up and be normal about it. Now I go to see bands, and constantly listen to music because that's what I love and always have, so why can't I do both? Why can't the two co-exist? I'm not out gigging, but I'm very comfortable with that now.

"There are things I've done that
I'm proud of and give me
a sense of achievement.
But that doesn't have to have
been selling a million records.
No more than I have to have
won Great British Menu.
It doesn't make me any less
proud of the time I had on it.
It's all good and it's all relative."

FILLET-OF-PLAICE, MUSSELS-AND-ALMONDS

IT DOESN'T HAVE TO BE PLAICE, BUT WHEN IT'S IN SEASON IT'S LOVELY, GOOD VALUE, AND YOU CAN GET A BIG FILLET. WHEN IT'S SMALLER IT'S BETTER ON THE BONE. BUT YOU COULD USE BRILL, JOHN DORY, OR TURBOT INSTEAD IF YOU ARE FEELING FLUSH

Ingredients: serves 4

Mussels

1 small onion, peeled and
    finely sliced
3 cloves of garlic, peeled
    and crushed
1 sprig of thyme
1 bay leaf
500g live mussels, scrubbed
    and de-bearded
250ml dry white wine

Almond milk

150ml mussel liquor
100g flaked almonds

4 fillets of plaice, roughly
    150g each, skinned
1 bunch of barba di frate
a knob of butter
fine sea salt
freshly ground white pepper

To cook the mussels, heat a little olive oil in a saucepan then sweat the onion and garlic. Add the herbs and the mussels. Turn up the heat, then add the wine and put a lid on. Leave to steam for a couple of minutes, shaking the pan occasionally.

Once all the mussels have opened, strain through a colander, making sure you collect all the mussel liquor in a bowl underneath.

Once the mussels are cool enough to handle, remove them from their shells.

To make the almond milk, pass the reserved mussel cooking liquor through a fine sieve, to remove any sand and grit. You should end up with about 150ml. Toast the flaked almonds until lightly golden, save a handful for garnish and put the rest in a small saucepan, along with the mussel liquor. Bring to just below boiling temperature, remove from the heat and cover with cling film. Leave to infuse for about 1 hour. Transfer to a blender and blitz for a few seconds. Strain through a fine sieve, making sure you squeeze out all the almond milk you can.

Spread the remaining almond mulch, from the sieve, on a tray and dry it out in a low oven. Using a spice grinder or powerful blender, grind the dried-out nuts with a pinch of salt and a tablespoonful of olive oil, until it forms a smooth paste.

To serve, heat a little vegetable oil in a frying pan, season the plaice fillets and fry until golden and crisp, and cooked about two-thirds through. Turn and continue to cook for 30 seconds.

Drop the barba di frate into salted boiling water for 1 minute, drain and toss in a knob of butter and white pepper.

Put the mussels in the almond milk and reheat until warm.

Spread a little of the almond paste onto your warm plates. Place the fish on top with the barba di frate. Put the mussels around and then using a hand blender, froth the remaining almond milk and spoon over the fish, scatter a few toasted flaked almonds over the top.

SIKA-DEER,MASHED-SWEDE, CHANTERELLES,TWIGLETS

Ingredients: serves 4

400g piece of venison loin
    (preferably sika), completely
    trimmed of all silver skin
a knob of butter
75g yellow chanterelles
1/2 clove of garlic, peeled
    and finely diced
kale or cabbage cress

Spiced damson sauce
450g damsons, stoned
550g soft brown sugar
350ml red wine vinegar
1 stick cinnamon
2.5g whole cloves
2.5g ground allspice
2.5g ground coriander seeds
2.5g ground ginger

Twiglets
75g plain flour
15g water
10g black treacle
5g olive oil
10g malt extract or treacle
10g Marmite

Pudding filling
300g diced venison
    (preferably sika), for braising
1 onion, peeled and finely diced
1 carrot, peeled and finely sliced
1 sprig of thyme
1 star anise
1 bay leaf
150ml red wine
300ml venison or chicken stock

Suet pastry
200g self-raising flour
100g suet
3g fine sea salt
1tsp chopped fresh thyme leaves
1 egg yolk
water

Mashed swede
1 small swede
15g sea salt
50g butter
freshly ground black pepper

To make the spiced damson sauce, put everything into a non-reactive pan, bring to the boil and simmer for 20 minutes, or until thick. Transfer to a blender and blend to a smooth shiny jam. Store in a squeezy bottle. This will keep in the fridge for ages.

To make the twiglets, mix the flour and water with the treacle. Once smooth work in the olive oil. Leave to rest for 30 minutes. Pinch off little pieces of the dough and roll them on your work surface with your hands into thin sticks. Lay them on a baking mat or parchment-lined tray and bake at 190°C for 5 minutes. Mix the malt extract or treacle with the Marmite (if it's too thick and sticky, blast it for a couple of seconds in the microwave) then lightly brush onto each twig to glaze. Sprinkle with salt flakes and leave in a very low oven or a hot cupboard for a couple of hours until crisp.

To make the pudding filling, in a small casserole or pressure cooker, brown the diced venison in a little oil or fat of your choice. Season with sea salt and freshly ground white pepper. Remove the meat then add the onion and sweat until soft. Add the carrot, thyme, bay leaf, star anise and red wine. Bring the wine to the boil for a few seconds before returning the meat and covering with the stock. Cover with a circle of parchment and a lid and cook in an oven at about 170°C for an hour-and-a-half or pressure cook at full tilt for 30 minutes. Leave to cool then strain through a sieve or colander. Chop the carrot into smallish pieces and mix with the meat and onion. Discard the thyme stalks, star anise and bay leaf. Reduce the remaining gravy to a sauce consistency; reserve enough for serving, mixing the remainder with the venison.

To make the suet pastry, mix everything together and add just enough cold water to bring it all together, but not so much that it becomes sticky. Butter and flour 4 individual pudding moulds. Roll out your pastry to about 2mm thick, using a pastry cutter cut 4 discs big enough to line the moulds and 4 smaller discs for the lids.

Line and fill the moulds with your braised venison mix, put on the lids, trim any excess pastry making sure the lids are sealed tightly. Wrap each pudding in cling film and steam for 30 minutes.

To make the mashed swede, peel and cut the swede into small chunks, cover with water, add salt and bring to the boil then simmer until very tender. Drain well before returning to the pan then roughly mash with the butter. Grind in plenty of black pepper.

Season the venison loin with fine sea salt and pan roast in a little oil over a moderately high heat for 3 or 4 minutes. Add a knob of butter and continue to cook for another couple of minutes whilst continually basting with the butter until rare. Leave to rest in a warm place for 10 minutes. Briefly sauté the chanterelles and garlic in a little butter until just wilted.

To serve, turn the puddings onto warm plates with a spoonful of swede on each. Carve the loin into 4 even pieces, season the cut surfaces before putting on the plates. Squeeze a few dots of damson sauce around then scatter the mushrooms and twiglets along with a few sprigs of kale cress. Warm the remaining venison sauce and pour over the puddings.

SIKA-DEER,MASHED-SWEDE, CHANTERELLES,TWIGLETS

SIKA DEER IS OF JAPANESE ORIGIN. IT'S JUST STUNNING, IT'S THE MOST BEAUTIFUL PIECE OF MEAT. THE IDEA IS THAT IT'S THE DEER AND THE FOREST FLOOR. IT'S AUTUMNAL, SO WE USE CHANTERELLES, AND A LITTLE BIT OF SWEETNESS AND SPICE COMES FROM THE DAMSONS

GRILLED-OCTOPUS,BEETROOT, FETA,ORANGE,OLIVE-SALT

Ingredients: serves 8

1 small octopus

Olive salt
12 Kalamata olives
20g Maldon sea salt

2 medium-sized beetroot
150g barrel-aged feta cheese,
    cut into cubes
2 oranges, peeled and segmented
a few sprigs of fennel
extra virgin olive oil

To cook the octopus, remove the tentacles and discard the body. Pressure cook the tentacles at full pressure with 150ml of water for 15 minutes. Leave to cool. To cook without a pressure cooker, cover the tentacles with water, bring to a boil and simmer for 45 minutes to an hour, or until tender. Remove from the pan and leave to cool.

Once cool, cover and chill the tentacles in the fridge until required.

To make the olive salt, remove the stones from the olives, cut into halves, spread onto a baking tray and dehydrate in a very low oven for a few hours, or until very dry and hard. Using a spice grinder or powerful blender, grind to a powder along with the Maldon salt.

To cook the beetroot, scrub the beets, wrap them in cling film or a vacuum pack bag then steam them for 4 hours. Light a barbecue, lay the beets on the hot coals and bake them for an hour, turning regularly to make sure they don't get too charred. When they are cool enough to handle, remove the black and charred exterior to reveal the sweet and smoky flesh. Cut into dice.

To serve, get the barbecue nice and hot, toss the octopus tentacles in a little olive oil then grill for a couple of minutes, until warm and charred.

Place a tentacle on each plate, with a couple of cubes of feta, beetroot and the orange segments. Place a little pile of olive salt on each plate, a few sprigs of fennel and a drizzle of olive oil.

USE THE BEST FETA POSSIBLE, PREFERABLY BARREL-AGED.
WE USE BLOOD ORANGES, AND MAKE THIS DISH WHEN THEY ARE
AROUND. ANY OTHER TIME OF YEAR JUST USE NORMAL ORANGES,
OR IT WOULD BE NICE WITH PINK GRAPEFRUIT

ROAST-DUCK-BREAST, MUSHROOM-TORTELLINI, LAPSANG-SOUCHONG

Ingredients: serves 6

6 duck breasts,
    roughly 200g each
maple syrup
fine sea salt and white pepper
a small handful of radish cress

Tortellini
5 free range egg yolks
1 whole free range egg
300g 00 flour
100g wild mushrooms
a knob of butter
1 clove of garlic
sea salt and white pepper
100g chicken breast
4 leaves of tarragon
100g whipping cream

Pickled turnips
2 large white turnips
100ml Moscatel vinegar
50ml dry white wine
50ml water
50g golden caster sugar
1 bay leaf
1 sprig of thyme
5g fine sea salt

Duck tea
trim and fillets from
    the duck breasts
mushroom trimmings
2 banana shallots, peeled
    and finely diced
500ml water
20g soy sauce
1 tsp Lapsang Souchong
    tea leaves

To prepare the duck breasts, remove the small fillets from each breast along with any sinews and all silver skin, reserve. Score the fat side into a diamond pattern.

To make the tortellini, make the pasta dough by adding the yolks and whole egg to the flour in a food processor. Pulse until it starts to look like coarse breadcrumbs. Turn onto a work surface and bring together with your hands. Wrap in cling film and leave to rest in the fridge for an hour.

Clean and trim the mushrooms, reserving any trimmings for the duck tea. Sauté the mushrooms in a knob of butter, grate in the garlic and season with fine sea salt and white pepper. Transfer to a tray to cool.

Put the chicken in a blender with a teaspoon of salt and blitz to a purée. Put the blender jug and chicken in the freezer for a few minutes to chill down. Add the tarragon and half the cream and continue to blitz until smooth. Be careful not to split the mix. Chill it again, and then rub the mousse through a sieve. Put the mousse into a cold bowl. Chill it again, then beat in the remaining cold cream by hand. Fold in the cooled mushrooms.

Cut your pasta dough in half (freeze the rest for another dish). Using a pasta machine, put the dough through the widest setting a few times, folding it back on itself each time. Carry on passing it through the machine adjusting the settings after each time, passing it through the finest setting twice.

Using a pastry cutter (approximately 10cm) cut discs from the pasta. Spoon some mushroom filling onto each disc. Spray or brush each disc with a little water then fold in half, making sure there are no air bubbles, seal the edges. Wrap each parcel around your finger and pinch the ends together.

Blanch the tortellini in boiling salted water for 1 minute then refresh in iced water. Drain and put on a covered tray in the fridge until required.

To make the pickled turnips, peel and cut each turnip into 3 round discs. Blanch in salted water until just tender, remove to a bowl. Bring all of the pickle ingredients to boil, cool for a few minutes before pouring over the turnips.

To make the duck tea, put all of the ingredients except the Lapsang into a pressure cooker. Cook at full pressure for an hour. Pass through a fine sieve into a saucepan. Add the tea and bring back to a boil. Taste to see if the Lapsang is strong enough and to check the seasoning, before straining into a small teapot.

Season the duck breasts and place skin side down into a dry frying pan, cook gently to render the fat and crisp the skin for about 10 minutes before turning and cooking for another 5 minutes. Add a good squirt of maple syrup and turn the breasts to glaze. Rest in a warm place for 10 minutes.

To serve, add the tea to the duck broth and bring back to a boil.

Put the tortellini into boiling salted water for 2 minutes, drain.

Warm the turnips and place one in the centre of each warm bowl.

Carve each breast and place next to the turnips. Put the tortellini on top, garnish with radish cress, and pour the tea over at the table.

PARMESAN-SHORTBREAD

Ingredients: makes 8-12 biscuits

150g plain flour
75g freshly grated parmesan
a pinch of cayenne pepper
100g butter
1 large free range egg yolk

To make the shortbread, put all the dry ingredients in a food processor and whiz to mix everything together. Add the butter and pulse to form a crumb. With the machine running, add egg yolk until it all comes together into a sticky dough. Using cling film, form into a large roll and put in the fridge to rest for about half an hour or until you need it.

Cut into neat discs about 5mm thick, arrange on a baking tray and bake at 180°C for 12 minutes. Cool the biscuits on a wire rack then store in an airtight container.

YOU COULD ALSO DO THESE WITH GOOD CHEDDAR OR A BLUE CHEESE. YOU DON'T HAVE TO BE A SLAVE TO THE CHEESE

GOAT'S-CHEESE
DIGESTIVE-CREAMS

Ingredients: makes 16 biscuits, with cheese left over for another use

Digestives
150g wholemeal flour
50g plain flour
3g baking powder
15g pinhead oatmeal
75g soft dark brown sugar
3g fine sea salt
100g butter
60ml milk

Goat's cheese cream
200g goat's cheese of your choice
75g mascarpone
salt and pepper to taste

To make the digestives, put all the dry ingredients into a food processor and whiz to mix everything together. Pulse in the butter to make a crumb then add milk until the dough comes together. Wrap in cling film and leave to rest in the fridge for half an hour or until required. Remove from fridge and leave until just soft enough to roll.

Line a board with baking parchment, roll the dough onto the parchment to a thickness of about 3mm then place in the fridge to firm up. Using a 4cm round pastry cutter, cut out as many biscuits as you can. Place them on a baking tray and bake at 180°C for 10 minutes or until golden. Cool on a wire rack and store in an airtight container until needed.

To make the goat's cheese cream, place everything in a food processor and blitz until smooth. Scrape the mix into a piping bag.

To serve, pipe a small amount of the cheese onto half of your biscuits and top with the other half.

YOU COULD MAKE BIGGER VERSIONS OF THE DIGESTIVES AND JUST DIP THEM IN YOUR TEA! OR ROLL IT OUT AND LINE A TART CASE OR MAKE A CHEESECAKE BASE

THE
WEST-HOUSE

WE'RE A SMALL TEAM, A FAMILY

"We've got Dad in the kitchen, with Mum and our son out front. I think that's quite rare in UK."

We tried to make it the four of us, Jess gave it a try but it wasn't for her. And until very recently I've only ever had one person helping me in the kitchen since that first year. When the kitchen team is that tiny, just you and one other, it really matters who they are. One guy Luke was great, but in the end he wanted to move on. I had another who ended up robbing me blind. Good riddance.

After he left I needed someone new, and I'd been sent a letter asking if I had any jobs going, from a guy called Ben Crittenden. I looked at the name and thought I recognised it. I already had his CV, he'd sent it a few years earlier, and for some reason I'd kept it. It was in a plastic folder by the phone, still waiting for me to ring him back. I called, and asked him if he'd applied before. And he said, "Yeah, when I was in college." I told him I still had his CV by the phone. It's a standing joke now, when I tell people I'll get back to them, but don't worry if you don't hear from me this week. Ben goes, "Yeah, might take five years!"

We had a chat, and then he came down to visit. But I was a bit reluctant with him. I was being very careful about who was coming in. I wanted things run properly, as close to perfect as we could get in our own little way, and I didn't know what he was going to be like. I said I needed someone to commit. It's too difficult with the way we work to have people chopping and changing. He said he'd commit. So that was it, but I was still reluctant.

He's been with me six years now. We work well together.

But when you get people like Ben on board, you've got a responsibility to them, they need to progress in their careers, in their knowledge, in everything they do, and surely my role is to facilitate that, otherwise they need to move on. He'd already been to other places and done stages and odds and sods. But you have to be able to let them progress somehow. When you're in a two-man situation like we've been, where does it go? If at some point in the future that involves him doing something on his own, which is most chefs' ultimate goal, I hope that I could help him with that and be a part of it.

Front of house, Jake's interest grew as he got more involved. It started off by him helping Jackie out and what has happened has evolved naturally. He's young, he's keen, he's learnt a lot, he has an interest, he goes to lots of restaurants, he looks at stuff. The biggest transition for him was getting into wine, because as a kid, he didn't like alcohol, even when we used to offer him a sip to try. He just didn't like it, ever. And Jackie always insisted he try it with the food, to see how different it tasted. But it wasn't for him.

Then one day we were doing a wine tasting with our rep, and I'd put things together for tasting menus, we were tasting certain dishes with potential wines. I remember, we had pigeon with a Faugères.

It went really well, it brought out the gameyness, you could almost taste that on the wine. An incredible wine, an incredible match, but a serious wine. When you're starting out with wines, you don't usually start with something like that. A wine like Faugères is pretty intense. Jake tasted it, having tasted the pigeon, and he got what we'd been talking about. It was a light bulb moment, he loved it, and he totally got it, and it was a big deal to him, it became his favourite wine. And then, as a result of that, he got into the other wines, and now he's all over it. He's been on various wine courses.

So he's ambitious, he's very like me. He gets frustrated if it's not right and if there's a problem. He wants people to like everything, and he wants the reviews to be good.

We're still a small team, so everyone does everything, it has to be that way. It's only now that we've got a few more bodies in the kitchen that it has been possible to develop things together, with that extra pair of hands. I had things I was trying to do before that I couldn't execute, not on my own. Like this dish called All The Fun of the Fair that we did shortly after Ben joined us. We had a toffee apple panna cotta in a glass jar, and it had a little apple sorbet on a stick dipped in a caramel, as a toffee apple. And we had candy floss on top of that. I wanted candy floss and Ben found one of those old toy candy floss machines in his mum's attic and he brought that in. And on the side we had a shot infused with popcorn. It tasted like Butterkist! We still get customers asking us about it. And that was over six years ago!

But the food changes. Everything I make I try and make better than the time before.

We're constantly evolving what we do, evolving the food, the menus, always looking at suppliers. I get excited by suppliers, produce, and finding things.

But essentially work is just a wheel going round and round. I think it's only when I look back that I realise how far I've come. When I look back to the day of opening with Jackie, I got open in three weeks from the day we got the keys, three-and-a-half to be precise. It was out of necessity, because of the loan.

You've got to meet your first month's payment. I didn't have the big payroll to wipe me out, I didn't have any payroll, that's how I survived. I scraped through. Otherwise, every day I'm thinking forward, thinking about the next thing, and the struggle of what we're doing now. Obviously, the more people I employ, the more crap I have to put up with. And every week there's a new health and safety issue or new legislation brought in which I don't have time to do, we're too small to deal with. And I'm paying so many different things and bills for services, for fuck-all at the end of the day. That's what it's like now.

I speak now for the entire nation of chefs of a calibre, of a level of restaurant, mainly Michelin, but not just Michelin. I don't believe there is one of us who would purposely ever send anything shite, just for the sake of it. No one! Because every one cares so passionately about what they're putting on the plate. We might get it wrong in a dish or a combination, we might get it wrong in other ways, but nothing is ever intentionally sent bad. If you don't enjoy the food, the cooking, the style of restaurant, that's fine, but don't come and criticise for the sake of it, it's our home, it's what we do. People say I take it personally. It is fucking personal.

Chefs can get cocky, and disappear up their own arses, but they don't realise they're up there. It's a real danger if you start to take yourself too seriously.

"We are not saving lives, it's only food. Everybody cooks, everybody has to eat. It's as simple as that. It's not rocket science. It's creative, but that's because we want to do that. It's still just food. You can beat yourself up, you can put a gun in your mouth and blow your head off because you think you're going to lose a star, even though you're not."

AT THE END OF THE DAY, WE'RE
JUST COOKING AND IT'S A JOB

But when you've got one small restaurant with a small margin it's a balancing act all the time. I'm not complaining, because we've done all right, and through tough times, even through recession, and I think TV and all those things obviously helped. There's a lot of luck involved, but there's a hell of a lot of hard work involved too, to make it happen and to sustain it, and to try and make the right decisions. You've always got to be on your game, every day. You can never be complacent about anything, not for a minute.

I'm not the first person to subscribe to the philosophy that you can't just reach a plateau, think you've arrived and now you have to sustain it. That's doesn't work, because there is no maintaining it. In my opinion, there are only two directions: you're either on your way up or you're on your way down. You are either trying to improve all the time, or if you stop doing that, then you're going down. You can't stay put, because even if you did stay exactly how you were and keep everything exactly perfect and the same, every day life changes, things evolve around you. You've got to evolve with them, you've always got to push forward. If you don't, if you're not constantly pushing forward, then you're going backwards. And it's inevitable where that ends up.

I believe that if you genuinely enjoy food and you live it and breathe it, then like most things, like if you're writing or drawing or writing a song or whatever, it's influenced by where your mind's at on a particular day or in a particular moment. If there is beautiful sunshine on a wintry day it creates a mood, it creates a feeling.

Therefore, if you were going out to eat on that day, before you've even looked at a menu, subconsciously you're probably thinking about what you fancy.

So I think that whatever mindset you're in, whatever you're craving that day, whatever you would like to eat, whatever your mood is, it's kind of what you want to be cooking.

You want to be doing what you enjoy. You should always cook what you enjoy eating. Some people say it's a pretentious, arsey chef who says he won't cook something because he doesn't like it, but I'm in that camp. I don't want to cook ingredients that I don't like. If I don't 100% feel it and believe in a dish or an ingredient, then I can't cook it well. I've no interest in cooking it.

I grew up eating, I grew up liking food, I read cookbooks, I had an interest, it was a hobby, and it stayed a hobby and an interest through my whole life. I then ended up doing it professionally to a high standard, to star level that a lot of people can't reach. I don't just do that and then go home and do something else, I live and breathe it 24 hours a day.

CONFIT-CEP,PARMESAN
GNOCCHI,ONION-BROTH

Ingredients: serves 8

4 large fresh ceps
300g duck fat
a few shavings of fresh parmesan
2 peeled cooked chestnuts
a small handful of chives

Gnocchi
1 large free range egg yolk
325g very dry warm mashed potato
5g fine sea salt
2g white pepper
75g 00 flour
20g parmesan, freshly grated

Onion broth
4 onions, peeled and
    roughly chopped
2g bicarbonate of soda
2 cloves garlic, peeled and crushed
3 sprigs of thyme
6 black peppercorns
35ml water
soy sauce

Wipe the ceps with a clean cloth and trim or scrape any dodgy bits from the stalks. Cut each cep in half lengthwise then lay them in a single layer in a pan or roasting tray. Cover them with the melted duck fat and keep over a very low heat for 20 minutes. You can now store the mushrooms in the fat until needed.

To make the gnocchi, using your hands, mix the egg yolk into the warm potato with salt and pepper. Gradually start working in the flour until you have a soft dough then work in the parmesan. Using a rolling pin, roll the dough to about 1cm thick then cut into 8 rounds with a pastry cutter. Poach the gnocchi in barely simmering salted water until they float to the surface. Drain them on a dry cloth.

To make the onion broth, put everything in a pressure cooker and cook for 20 minutes. Strain through muslin, leaving until it stops dripping. Season with soy sauce.

To serve, drain the ceps from the fat and fry on each side until nicely caramelised. Keep them warm while you fry each gnocchi in a little of the strained duck fat, which will have now taken on the most amazing mushroom flavour. Place a fried gnocchi in each warm bowl, top each with a cep half and a few shavings of fresh parmesan. Pour the broth around then finish by grating the chestnut over the top and garnish with chives.

WE DO ONE BIG GNOCCHI, BUT IF YOU WANT TO DO MORE
TRADITIONAL SHAPES, OR WHATEVER YOUR GNOCCHI
SKILLS RUN TO, GO FOR IT. IF YOU DON'T HAVE CEPS,
BAKED FIELD MUSHROOMS WOULD BE NICE

CATALAN-TRIFLE

CREMA CATALANA MEETS ENGLISH TRIFLE. ROUND YOUR NAN'S YOU WOULD HAVE A PROPER SHERRY TRIFLE. SHERRY IS SPANISH, SO IT GOT ME THINKING. I REDID A TRIFLE WITH SPANISH ELEMENTS. BUT THE BEST TOPPING TURNED OUT TO BE LIKE A TIRAMISU WITH MASCARPONE

Ingredients: serves 8

Trifle sponge
4 large free range eggs, separated
100g golden caster sugar
100g plain flour
1/2 tsp baking powder

Sherry jelly
200ml water
2 leaves gelatine, soaked in
    cold water to bloom
200ml Pedro Ximénez sherry

Catalan custard
150g milk
450ml whipping cream
2 sticks of cinnamon
8g fennel seeds
pinch of saffron strands
zest of 1/2 an orange
zest of 1 lemon
8 large free range egg yolks
65g golden caster sugar
2 leaves of gelatine, soaked in
    cold water to bloom

Trifle topping
2 large free range eggs
140g golden caster sugar
250g mascarpone
240g whipping cream
toasted flaked almonds

Cinnamon tuille
50g soft butter
110g icing sugar
110g plain flour
5g ground cinnamon
100g egg white

To make the trifle sponge, whisk the egg whites until they start to thicken. Add 2 tablespoons of sugar and continue to whisk until soft peak stage.

In a separate bowl, whisk the egg yolks with the rest of the sugar until pale and fluffy. Gently fold them together, followed by the flour and baking powder. Spread the mix evenly onto a lined baking tray and bake for 8 minutes at 200°C.

When evenly golden, remove from the baking tray, turn it upside down and peel away the parchment whilst still warm.

Leave to cool before cutting into discs to fit the base of your trifle glasses.

To make the sherry jelly, heat 100ml of the water, squeeze the excess liquid from the gelatine then add to the water to melt. Remove from the heat and whisk in the rest of the water and the sherry. Pour a little into the bottom of each glass.

Place a disc of sponge in each. Leave it to set just enough to stop the sponge from floating before adding the rest of the jelly. Put them in the fridge to set.

For the Catalan custard, bring the milk, cream and all the flavourings to just below the boil. Whisk the yolks and sugar together and then whisk in the hot liquid. Squeeze the excess water from the gelatine and stir into the custard. Make sure it's all dissolved before passing through a fine sieve into a jug.

Leave to cool before pouring over the jelly. Make sure it's not too warm or it will melt the jelly rather than setting in layers. Return them to the fridge.

To make the trifle topping, whisk the eggs and the sugar to a light sabayon. Whisk the mascarpone and cream together. Add to the sabayon and continue to whisk to a smooth thick cream. Transfer to a piping bag.

Pipe the cream onto the custard in whatever pattern you fancy then return them to the fridge until ready to serve.

For the cinnamon tuille, put the butter and sugar in a food processor and whiz until smooth. Add the flour and cinnamon, followed by the egg white.

Spread the mix in circles on a lined baking sheet as thinly as possible and bake at 175°C for about 7 minutes, or until evenly coloured.

Working from the oven to keep them warm, one at a time peel them from the tray and wrap tightly around the handle of a wooden spoon so they resemble cinnamon sticks.

To serve, scatter a few toasted flaked almonds over the trifles and top with a cinnamon tuille.

CRUNCHIE,
CHOCOLATE-SORBET

Ingredients: serves 4

Chocolate moulds
200g dark chocolate

Honeycomb
50g golden caster sugar
40g golden syrup
5g bicarbonate of soda

Parfait
50g water
50g golden caster sugar
2 free range egg yolks
90g white chocolate
175ml whipping cream

Chocolate sorbet
100g golden caster sugar
2g stabilizer - Louis François
    Stab 2000
325g water
100g Valrhona Guanaja
    chocolate, 70%
50g cocoa powder

To make the chocolate moulds, you will need flexible moulds to freeze the bars. Start by melting the dark chocolate and using a brush coat the insides of the mould, trying not to leave any gaps. Put them in the fridge for a few minutes to set before giving a second coat. Put them back in the fridge until needed.

To make the honeycomb, put the sugar and syrup into a saucepan and cook to a very dark caramel. Remove from the heat and whisk in the bicarbonate of soda. As it turns pale and foamy, tip it onto a baking mat or parchment and leave to cool.

To make the parfait, start by boiling the water and sugar together to make syrup. Put the egg yolks into the bowl of an electric mixer then whisk in the boiling syrup and continue whisking to a thick white sabayon. Melt the white chocolate and 50ml of whipping cream, and fold into the cooled sabayon. In a clean bowl, whisk the 125ml of the cream to a soft peak before folding into the mixture.

Smash up the honeycomb and fold as much as you like into the parfait (you won't need it all), save what's left to garnish.

Spoon the mix into your chocolate-coated moulds, smoothing them off as you go. Freeze them for at least 4 hours or until required.

To make the chocolate sorbet, mix the sugar and stabiliser in a pan. Add the water and bring to the boil. Pour over the chocolate and cocoa to melt, then using a hand blender whiz to emulsify. Chill it in the fridge overnight. Blitz again before churning in your ice cream machine.

To serve, carefully push the crunchies from the moulds and serve alongside a scoop of sorbet topped with a sprinkling of the leftover honeycomb.

I GOT THE WHITE CHOCOLATE PARFAIT AND THE HONEYCOMB ALL
SORTED. THEN BEN CAME IN WITH SILICONE MOULDS AND TRIED
TO DO IT IN A SHELL. IT REALLY WORKED, HE CRACKED IT.
ONCE I ADDED THE CHOCOLATE SORBET IT WAS GOOD TO GO

MILK-AND-HONEY

i WAS WATCHING TElly ON A SATURDAY MORNING, EATING A BOWl
OF HONEY NUT ClUSTERS, AND THINKING ABOUT THE CHEWY BITS,
THE CRUNCH AND THE MilK. i WANTED TO DO A DiSH BASED ON THAT.
AFTER A FAIR BIT OF WORK AND iDEAS WE CAME UP WITH THiS

Ingredients: serves 6

Buttermilk ice cream
150g golden caster sugar
3g stabiliser - Louis François
  Stab 2000
550ml buttermilk,
  see page 26
pinch of salt
juice of 1/2 lemon

Milk crisps
85g whole milk
20g milk powder

Milk jelly
50g whipping cream
140g whole milk
50g raw honey
0.6g iota carrageenan

Milk mousse
1 leaf gelatine, soaked in cold
  water to bloom
150g whipping cream
25g golden caster sugar
1 vanilla pod
350g whole milk

Nuggets
25g plain flour
40g milk powder
5g cornflour
pinch of salt
15g golden caster sugar
25g butter, melted
50g white chocolate, melted

a few spoonfuls of dulce de leche

To make the buttermilk ice cream, mix the sugar and stabiliser together then heat until dissolved. Add the buttermilk, salt and lemon then whiz with a hand blender. Leave overnight in the fridge, blitz again before churning in your ice cream machine.

To make the milk crisps, mix the milk and milk powder together, pour onto a non-stick baking mat or parchment lined tray. Bake on your oven's lowest setting until completely dry and crisp. Break into rough shards then store in an airtight container.

To make the milk jelly, line the base of 6 mousse rings very tightly with cling film and place them on a flat tray. Put all the jelly ingredients into a pan. Using a hand blender, whiz to make sure the iota is dispersed. Heat the pan to 80°C then pour into rings. Leave them to cool before refrigerating.

To make the milk mousse, soak the gelatine in cold water to bloom. Heat the cream, sugar and seeds from the vanilla pod. Squeeze excess water from the gelatine and add to cream. Make sure everything has completely dissolved before removing from the heat and adding the milk. Pour into a cream siphon and charge, shake well then store it in the fridge.

To bake the nuggets, set your oven to 150°C. In a bowl, mix the flour, 25g of the milk powder, cornflour, salt and sugar together, add the melted butter and mix until it all starts to clump together.

Squeeze the clumps into little nugget-sized pieces and place on a baking mat or parchment-lined tray. Bake for around 15-20 minutes or until lightly golden. Leave to cool completely then toss them in the remaining milk powder, making sure they're evenly coated. Don't worry if some of them crumble a bit. Melt the white chocolate in a bowl then tip them into it and stir them around, again making sure they are evenly coated. Spread them evenly on a tray then chill them in the fridge until the chocolate has set. Store in an airtight container.

To serve, turn out the jellies onto your plates. Add a few dots of dulce de leche and a few milk nuggets, and a scoop of ice cream.

Carefully squirt your mousse on top of the jelly and decorate with a few crisps.

Ingredients: serves 8

Pressed apple
10 Cox's Orange Pippin or
    Braeburn apples
50g butter, melted
5g pectin (optional)

Elderberry sorbet
250g elderberries
100ml water
25g liquid glucose
75g golden caster sugar
2g super neutrose stabiliser
1/2 leaf gelatine, soaked in cold
    water to bloom
10ml lemon juice

Cobnut cream
100g cobnuts, roasted and skinned
100ml milk
150ml whipping cream
3 large free range egg yolks
50g golden caster sugar
10g cornflour

Brambles
40 brambles
50g golden caster sugar
1 tsp water

Cobnut crumble
100g plain flour
30g muscovado sugar
50g golden caster sugar
40g skinned chopped cobnuts
20g jumbo oats
a pinch of ground cinnamon
80g butter

wild sorrel leaves

To make the pressed apple, peel and core the apples. Slice them very thinly on a mandoline. In a bowl, toss them in the melted butter and pectin (if using). Line a small terrine mould or 500g loaf tin with parchment paper. Layer the apples neatly and evenly in the tin. Cover with foil and bake at 180°C for 1 hour. Remove the foil and replace with a piece of parchment. Press the apples down before returning to the oven. Continue to cook for another hour or until lightly coloured and completely soft. Leave to cool a little before placing a weight on top, to press, and putting them in the fridge.

To make the sorbet, put the elderberries, water and glucose into a saucepan. Bring to a simmer. Mix the sugar with the stabiliser and add to the fruit mixture to dissolve. Transfer the fruit to a blender and blitz to a smooth purée. Squeeze the excess water from the gelatine before adding to the purée along with the lemon juice. Pass the mixture through a fine sieve. Leave to cool before churning in your ice cream machine.

To make the cobnut cream, bring the cobnuts, milk and cream to the boil, simmer for 5 minutes. Remove from the heat and cover the pan with cling film. Leave to infuse for 1 hour. Whisk the yolks, sugar and cornflour together until pale, Add the cobnut milk mixture and whilst stirring, bring back to the boil. Simmer for 2 minutes until thickened before blending to a smooth cream. Pass through a fine sieve and store in the fridge in a piping bag or squeezy bottle.

To heat the brambles, put the berries, sugar and water into a saucepan and warm them until they just start to soften and release their juice. Be careful not to let them get too soft and mushy.

To make the cobnut crumble, mix all the dry ingredients together and using your fingers, rub the butter in to the mixture, leaving it fairly lumpy. Spread evenly on to a lined baking tray and bake for 12 minutes at 180°C or until crisp and golden.

To serve, turn out the apple, remove the parchment and cut into neat slices. Place a slice on each plate with 5 brambles and a few dots of cobnut cream. Put a scoop of sorbet on top of the apple, sprinkle the crumble and garnish with a few wild sorrel leaves.

OUT THE BACK OF THE RESTAURANT WE HAVE
ELDERFLOWER BUSHES, WILD BRAMBLES AND CRAB APPLES.
WE HAVE COBNUTS TOO, WE ARE SURROUNDED BY THEM IN KENT,
SO WE THOUGHT WE'D DO A DISH WITH THEM ALL

RHUBARB-RISOTTO,SORBET, WHITE-CHOCOLATE-PARMESAN

THIS IS MY CREAMED RICE AND FRUIT TAKE ON RISOTTO.
THE CHOCOLATE IS TEMPERED AND MOULDED LIKE A PIECE OF
PARMESAN, AND THEN GRATED ALL OVER THE DISH WHEN THE
RISOTTO IS SERVED, FOLLOWED BY GRATED NUTMEG FROM A
PEPPER MILL - ITALIAN TRATTORIA-STYLE

Ingredients: serves 6

Rhubarb sorbet
3g super neutrose stabiliser
150g sugar
50g water
50g liquid glucose
3g dried hibiscus flowers
450g forced Yorkshire rhubarb,
    trimmed
pinch of sea salt

White chocolate parmesan
200g good quality white chocolate

Rhubarb
600g forced Yorkshire rhubarb,
    trimmed
275g golden caster sugar
2 strips of orange zest
5g dried hibiscus flowers
300ml water

Creamed rice
200g arborio rice
enough water to just cover the rice
1 litre whole milk
570ml whipping cream
4 vanilla pods
125g light soft brown sugar

fresh nutmeg, grated
a small handful of buckler
    leaf sorrel

To make the rhubarb sorbet, mix the stabliser and sugar to disperse, then dissolve in a non-reactive pan with the water, glucose and hibiscus. Chop the washed rhubarb into small pieces and add to the pan with a pinch of salt. Cover and simmer gently, stirring occasionally until the rhubarb has broken down. Leave to cool and blend to a smooth purée. Chill it in the fridge overnight, and then blend again before churning it in your ice cream machine, and then put in the freezer.

To make the chocolate parmesan, melt the chocolate over a bain-marie or defrost in the microwave. To temper the chocolate heat to 45-50°C, then on a marble slab or steel table, bring the temperature down to 26-27°C, then heat back up to 28-29°C. Or, if you prefer, you can skip the tempering and just melt the chocolate.

Pour the tempered, or melted, chocolate into a plastic container small enough to make it look like a piece of cheese when it sets. Put it in the fridge to set. Once set push it out of the plastic and wrap one end in aluminium foil.

To cook the rhubarb, trim the rhubarb stalks then cut them into even pieces of about 4cm, lay them evenly in one layer in a baking tray. Put the sugar, zest, hibiscus and water into a pan and bring to a boil. Pour the resulting syrup over the rhubarb. You can either put the tray over the heat or into a moderately hot oven, around 200°C for a few minutes or just until the rhubarb starts to soften. Leave to cool in the syrup. Remove the poached rhubarb pieces before straining the resulting juices into a small pan. Reduce until a viscous syrup is achieved. This can now be kept in a plastic squeezy bottle.

To make the creamed rice, put the rice into a medium-sized saucepan with just enough water to cover. Bring to the boil then immediately drain and rinse under cold water. Return to the saucepan and pour in the milk and cream. Split the vanilla pods and scrape out the seeds, add these along with the pods. Bring to a gentle simmer, stirring all the time to prevent it from catching on the bottom of the pan then continue to cook, stirring occasionally until the rice feels soft and the mixture resembles rice pudding. This should take at least half an hour. Add the sugar and carry on cooking and stirring until you have a very loose risotto consistency. Remove the vanilla pods then pour onto a tray to cool.

To serve, spoon the rice onto the middle of a plate, spreading it evenly to resemble a risotto. Squirt some of the syrup over the rice in whatever fashion suits. Top with a few pieces of poached rhubarb and a scoop, or quenelle, of sorbet. Serve to your guests, then holding the foil to stop it melting, grate the white chocolate over, and top with a little grated nutmeg. Garnish with buckler leaf sorrel.

TREACLE-TART

Ingredients: serves 8

Pastry
450g plain flour
150g icing sugar
zest of an orange
225g cold salted butter, diced
1 large free range egg
1 tbsp milk

Tart filling
275g golden syrup
25g black treacle
85g brioche or breadcrumbs
60 almonds, ground
1 large free range egg
150ml whipping cream
zest of an orange

blood orange segments
crème fraîche
a small handful of buckler
    leaf sorrel

To make the pastry, put the flour, icing sugar and orange zest into a food processor. Give it a whiz to mix, and then add the butter. Pulse until the mix resembles breadcrumbs. Add the egg and milk then pulse again until it just comes together. Make sure you don't overwork it. Turn the pastry out onto a work surface. Shape it into a ball. Flatten it then wrap in cling film. Leave it to rest in the fridge for an hour.

To make the filling, gently warm the syrup and treacle to make it easier to work with, then put all the ingredients into a blender and whiz until emulsified.

Roll out the pastry as thinly as possible. Cut out eight circles of pastry big enough to fit 8 small tartlet tins. Line with cling film or parchment paper. Fill with rice or baking beans, then blind bake for 10 minutes at 180°C.

Fill each tartlet case with the filling mix and bake for 15 minutes at 170°C.

To serve, place a warm tartlet in the centre of a plate. Arrange a few orange segments on each tart and finish with a spoon of crème fraîche and garnish with buckler leaf sorrel.

THIS IS BEN'S GO-TO TREACLE TART RECIPE, ONE OF THE FIRST THINGS HE DID WHEN HE STARTED. WE MAKE THEM INDIVIDUALLY, THE BEAUTY OF WHICH IS THAT WE CAN COOK THEM TO ORDER, SO THEY'RE HOT, FRESH AND CRISPY

CHOCOLATE-ORANGE

WE PUT THE CHOCOLATE CREAM IN A SHELL. HAZELNUT, CHOCOLATE, ORANGE, COFFEE, ALL FLAVOURS THAT ALL GO WELL TOGETHER. BUT IF YOU ARE NOT INTO ANY OF THOSE ELEMENTS LEAVE THEM OUT, OR MAKE IT ALL COFFEE, OR ALL ORANGE

Ingredients: serves 8

Chocolate domes
200g dark chocolate, 70%
50g bitter orange marmalade

Coffee cream
150ml whole milk
250ml whipping cream
2 strips of orange zest
50g golden caster sugar
5 large free range egg yolks
60g very strong espresso
40g Tia Maria
1 leaf gelatine, soaked in cold
    water to bloom
190g dark chocolate, 70%

Blood orange sorbet
8g super neutrose stabiliser
75g golden caster sugar
150g dextrose
zest of 2 oranges
200g water
500g blood orange juice
50g lemon juice

Chocolate crumb
35g plain flour
5g cocoa powder
35g ground almonds
35g golden caster sugar
pinch of salt
35g butter

Hazelnut butter
125g toasted skinned hazelnuts

Candied hazelnuts
110g golden caster sugar
60g water
60g blanched hazelnuts, skinned

Coffee syrup
50g golden caster sugar
150g strong espresso

To make the chocolate domes, you will need flexible moulds. Start by melting the dark chocolate. Using a brush coat the insides of the moulds with the chocolate, trying not to leave any gaps. Put them in the fridge for a few minutes to set before giving a second coat. Put them back in the fridge until needed.

To make the coffee cream, bring the milk, cream and orange zest to the boil. Whisk the sugar and yolks together. Add the espresso and Tia Maria, and then whisk in the hot milk and cream, put back on the heat and cook to 82°C. Add the gelatine. Melt the chocolate and using a hand blender, blend in to mixture. Pass through a fine sieve and leave to cool. When cold, transfer to a piping bag.

Spoon a little marmalade into the middle of each chocolate dome, and then fill them with the cream. Store in the fridge.

To make the blood orange sorbet, mix the stabiliser, sugar and dextrose. Add the zest and water then bring to the boil. Leave to cool completely then stir in the orange and lemon juice. Chill it in the fridge overnight, pass through a sieve to remove the zest then whiz with a hand blender before churning in your ice cream machine.

To make the chocolate crumb, mix all the dry ingredients then rub in the butter to form a rough crumble. Leave to rest in the fridge for about half an hour. Form into clumps onto a baking tray and bake at 160°C for about 15 minutes.

To make the hazelnut butter, blitz the nuts in a blender until a smooth paste is obtained.

To make the candied hazeluts, heat 60g of the sugar and the water to make a syrup. Add the hazelnuts and simmer for 5 minutes. Remove the nuts and add the rest of the sugar. Put the nuts back in the pan and continue simmering for another 5 minutes. Put the nuts onto a lined oven tray and bake at 170°C for 10 minutes.

For the coffee syrup, add the sugar to the espresso and simmer until a syrupy consistency is achieved.

To serve, spread a little hazelnut butter on the plate. Drizzle some coffee syrup around. Place a few chocolate crumbs in a line and sprinkle some candied nuts between them. Carefully turn out a chocolate dome onto each plate and place a scoop of sorbet alongside.

RECIPE-INDEX

IBERICO-PORK-PRESA,RAZOR CLAMS,WILD-GARLIC BUTTER/132

JOHN-DORY,CAULIFLOWER, ONION-BHAJI,CURRY-OIL/112

MISO-GLAZED-MACKEREL, SPICED-CUCUMBER,-YUZU MAYONNAISE/100

OLIVE-OIL-BRAISED CUTTLEFISH,PEAS,IBERICO HAM/116

ORGANIC-SALMON,PASTILLA, BULGAR,PEPPER,BABA GANOUSH/208

POACHED-OYSTERS,CHORIZO CREAM,CUCUMBER-GRANITA/206

ROAST-SCALLOPS,WILD GARLIC-PESTO/134

ROCKPOOL/102

SPICED-MACKEREL-KEBAB, AUBERGINE-CHUTNEY, TAHINI-SAUCE/38

TARAMASALATA/42

WARM-SMOKED-HADDOCK,BACON DRESSING,PEA-SHOOTS/28

FRUIT

BANANA-CAKE/50

CURED-FOIE-GRAS,DUCK CONFIT,PICKLED-RHUBARB, GINGERBREAD/220

GRAPPA-MARINATED PEACHES,LEMON-VERBENA, MASCARPONE/224

GRILLED-OCTOPUS,BEETROOT, FETA,ORANGE,OLIVE-SALT/248

HAZELNUT-AND-RAISIN BREAD/198

HEDGEROW/272

MELON-AND-HAM-GAZPACHO/40

RHUBARB-RISOTTO,SORBET, WHITE-CHOCOLATE PARMESAN/274

ROAST-SUCKLING-PIG,BAKED APPLE,BLACK-PUDDING/80

GAME

CHORIZO-CRUSTED-RABBIT, SMOKED-PEPPER-KETCHUP/78

PICKLED-PIGEON,NETTLE QUINOA/118

SIKA-DEER,MASHED-SWEDE, CHANTERELLES,TWIGLETS/244

STEAMED-HARE-BUN, CHOCOLATE-SAUCE/136

GRAINS

OATCAKES/226

ORGANIC-SALMON, PASTILLA,BULGAR,PEPPER, BABA-GANOUSH/208

PICKLED-PIGEON,NETTLE QUINOA/118

ICE-CREAM

CHOCOLATE-ORANGE/278

CRUNCHIE,CHOCOLATE SORBET/268

HEDGEROW/272

MILK-AND-HONEY/270

RECIPE-INDEX

ROAST-DUCK-BREAST,
MUSHROOM-TORTELLINI,
LAPSANG-SOUCHONG/250

PUDDINGS

CATALAN-TRIFLE/266

CHOCOLATE-ORANGE/278

CRUNCHIE,CHOCOLATE
SORBET/268

GRAPPA-MARINATED
PEACHES,LEMON-VERBENA,
MASCARPONE/224

HEDGEROW/272

MILK-AND-HONEY/270

RHUBARB-RISOTTO,SORBET,
WHITE-CHOCOLATE
PARMESAN/274

TREACLE-TART/276

RICE

OXTAIL-RISOTTO/204

RHUBARB-RISOTTO,SORBET,
WHITE-CHOCOLATE
PARMESAN/274

SOUPS

MELON-AND-HAM-GAZPACHO/40

VEGETABLES

ASPARAGUS-CARBONARA/148

BEETROOT-CHEESECAKE/178

CHORIZO-CRUSTED-RABBIT,
SMOKED-PEPPER-KETCHUP/78

CONFIT-CEP,PARMESAN
GNOCCHI,ONION-BROTH/264

FILLET-OF-HAKE,WILD
GARLIC-CROQUETAS,HAM
EMULSION/200

GRILLED-OCTOPUS,BEETROOT,
FETA,ORANGE,OLIVE-SALT/248

IBERICO-PORK-PRESA,
RAZOR-CLAMS,WILD-GARLIC
BUTTER/132

IRISH-COFFEE,CEP-AND
PARMESAN-DOUGHNUTS/228

JOHN-DORY,CAULIFLOWER,
ONION-BHAJI,CURRY-OIL/112

LAMB-BACON,SWEETBREAD,
PEAS/44

MISO-GLAZED-MACKEREL,
SPICED-CUCUMBER,YUZU
MAYONNAISE/100

OLIVE-OIL-BRAISED
CUTTLEFISH,PEAS,IBERICO
HAM/116

ORGANIC-SALMON,PASTILLA,
BULGAR,PEPPER,BABA
GANOUSH/208

PICKLED-ONIONS/58

POACHED-OYSTERS,CHORIZO
CREAM,CUCUMBER-GRANITA/206

ROAST-DUCK-BREAST,
MUSHROOM-TORTELLINI,
LAPSANG-SOUCHONG/250

ROAST-SCALLOPS,WILD
GARLIC-PESTO/136

SIKA-DEER,MASHED-SWEDE,
CHANTERELLES,TWIGLETS/244

SPICED-MACKEREL-KEBAB,
AUBERGINE-CHUTNEY,TAHINI
SAUCE/38

WARM-SMOKED-HADDOCK,BACON
DRESSING,PEA-SHOOTS/28

CREDITS

GRAHAM GARRETT

Graham's defection to cooking may be music's loss but it's the food world's gain.

He has worked for both Nico Ladenis and Richard Corrigan, as head chef of multiple restaurants. He has cooked for government and royalty, having been fortunate enough to cook at both 10 Downing Street, and also to cater a private dinner for Her Majesty, the Queen of England.

Graham and Jackie bought The West House in 2002 to create their own dining room, and allow Graham to pursue his own vision. Graham's food has gained the restaurant multiple awards, including a Michelin star.

Graham is most likely to be found in his kitchen, creating wonderful food.

CAT BLACK

Cat is a freelance food writer, and you can always find her in the kitchen at parties.

A member of The Guild of Food Writers and Grand Jury member of The International Chocolate Awards, she has written for a variety of publications, including The Spectator's Scoff and 1001 Restaurants You Must Experience Before You Die (Octopus). Due to Cat's passion for all that is finest in the world of chocolate, she not only writes about it, but gives talks about it and acts as a chocolate consultant.

Sharing delicious food is one of her best things in life. So hanging out with chefs is a welcome occupational hazard. There have been many happy hours spent at The West House.

ADRIAN FRANKLIN

Adrian's love for photography is life-long and has seen him go from process and printing - turning any available cupboard into a darkroom - to embracing the digital age.

He has more than 20 years of professional experience in the field. He cut his teeth at Time Out and City Limits, bombing around London on a motorbike with a camera bags and tripods strapped to the side. Corporate design, advertising and editorial work saw him focusing on portraiture. Photographing chefs he has found a mutual creative respect, which also gives him the opportunity to make some great still life imagery of food. Adrian runs Hospitality Media, which provides services specifically to all sectors of the hospitality and associated industries.

Working with Graham has meant a happy immersion in the contemplation of some very photogenic food.

SPECIAL THANKS

I really need to say a massive thank you to a lot of people for making many things possible. So in no particular order:

Jackie, Jake and Jess, Mum and Dad, Terry Stevens, Sam Blue and Ray Callcut (the boys in the band), Freddie Ball, Phil Collen, Jeff Hepting, Pete Webb, Andy Ives, Charles Campion, Jori White, Christoph Brooke, Jennifer Sharp, Richard Corrigan, Malcolm Starmer, Phil Jones, James Dew from Harwoods, Ben Crittenden, Anthony Hodgson, Adrian Franklin and Cat Black.

Archive photography mostly by Clifford Garrett.

Dinnerware mainly by Alan and Billy from Aylesford Pottery.

Anyone not on this list that probably should be...

I thank you all
Graham x